Vollenhoven's Problem-Historical Method

Introduction and Explorations

Vollenhoven's Problem-Historical Method

Introduction and Explorations

Kornelis A. Bril

Translated by Ralph W. Vunderink

Dordt College Press

Published with financial support from the Foundation "Pro Religione et Libertate" and under the auspices of the D.H.Th. Vollenhoven Foundation

For more information, contact the
Association for Reformational Philosophy:
Post Office Box 2156
3800CD Amersfoort, The Netherlands

Vollenhoven Newsletter No. 1 July 2003– . Email journal
Email: reform.philos@wxs.nl
Website: http://comte.to/reform.philosophy

Original title and publication: K. A. Bril "Probleemhistorische verken-ningen." Being Part II of A. Tol en K. A. Bril *Vollenhoven als wijsgeer. Inleidingen en teksten.* Amsterdam, Buijten en Schipperheijn, 1992.

All references to Holy Scripture are taken from the Revised Standard Version (RSV) unless otherwise noted.

Printed in the United States of America.

Dordt College Press   www.dordt.edu/dordt_press
498 Fourth Avenue NE
Sioux Center, Iowa 51250
United States of America

ISBN: 978-0-932914-60-6

The Library of Congress Cataloging-in-Publication Data
is on file with the Library of Congress, Washington, D.C.
Library of Congress Control Number: 2005927859

Contents

Part Four: Time-Currents

INTRODUCTION

In this preface, we intend to assist the reader with understanding Vollenhoven's problem-historical method by giving a concise overview of this method and its influence on Reformational philosophy. In the four parts of this work, a number of excursions will be made into this method as Vollenhoven applies it historically.

As we survey Western intellectual history, we can interpret the landscape in several ways. We can seek to capture, for its own sake, the wisdom of past accomplishments—for instance, the marvel of the ancient Parthenon, built during the fifth century B.C. in Athens. We can also try to discover their relevance for us today; we may appreciate the effect of the Italian painter Titian on the Flemish painter Rubens, the Romantic painter Turner, and the Impressionist painter Monet. We can even ask our predecessors to solve some of our contemporary problems; from the reign of terror during the French Revolution, we may learn how to cope with terrorism today. These and many other examples clearly show there are at least three ways of viewing historical connections.

A unique way of interpreting the history of philosophy has been provided by the late Dirk H. Th. Vollenhoven (1892–1978). But before introducing this original Dutch philosopher, let us give a concise summary of his historiographic view before elucidating the various aspects of his position in the body of the text.

A. VOLLENHOVEN: THE PROBLEM-HISTORICAL METHOD

Shortly after completing his graduate studies in 1918, Vollenhoven commenced his search for a clear direction, a reliable road map, in his orientation in the history of philosophy.[1] That project turned out to be a more demanding task than he had originally anticipated. In about 1940, after five unsatisfactory attempts and already having reached his fifties, he came across a more satisfactory method, which he tested and adopted in 1945. A few years later, in 1950, he designated his new way

---

1. Klaas J. Popma, Professor of Philosophy at the University in Utrecht and Groningen, typified Vollenhoven's work as making maps, clarifying historical links between philosophers (1941, 50).

"the problem-historical method" (1941k, 65, note 2; 1950e, 6). Once he had come to embrace his prized discovery, he persisted in perfecting it. He continued to work on it even in his retirement years, until he was obligated to lay his labors aside due to his advancing age and his declining mental powers three years before his death in 1978.

The core of Vollenhoven's problem-historical method can be summarized in one phrase: "seeing . . . an author and showing him to others in the light of the whole" (1961c, 34). This means that a historical thinker is related vertically to his predecessors and successors, as well as horizontally to his contemporaries. John Dewey, for instance, stands in a Darwinian tradition (see p. 31), and, in turn, is influenced by contemporary pragmatists like Charles Peirce and William James.

Types and Time-Currents

Vollenhoven explained the historical connections between certain thinkers by means of a crucial distinction between types and time-currents.

The term *types* concerns the place that humans occupy in the cosmos. In the Darwinian tradition, for instance, there is a phrase, "the animals, for instance, humans." Humans, it is true, have a certain biotic aspect: they are built up of cells with chromosomes and DNA, and, like animals, they have blood circulation and nervous systems. But should one claim, "primates (the great apes), for instance, humans," then one implies an ontological view of human nature, namely, animalism, which is a specific viewpoint that many protagonists since Darwin have ardently proclaimed. In addition to animalism, there are several other so-called types, or philosophical traditions, such as materialism, Thomism, and Gnosticism.

Vollenhoven used *time-currents* to pertain to the norms and their criteria that a thinker shares with his contemporaries. During the Kantian era (c. 1800), for instance, the widely prevailing view of human autonomy, or human reason, was as the determinant of the norms for good and evil. That is, intellectuals did not deem God's Word a law to themselves (theonomy) but considered it only an alien and oppressive set of rules (heteronomy). As they saw it, they could concur with this view only insofar as it agrees with the criteria concerning autonomy, or self-rule.

Thinkers of the succeeding period (the positivists) began to doubt the content of autonomous knowledge; there are, so they said, merely autonomous methods to acquire certain knowledge. Still later, Nietzsche claimed that there are no norms—neither rational nor divine. These three examples illustrate that human interpretations of norms differ from one period to the next.

Vollenhoven's problem-historical method, then, deals with thinkers both in their relation to their predecessors and followers (types) and to their contemporaries (time-currents).[2] In other words, types concern a view of ontology (e.g., humans are nothing but a configuration of matter), and time-currents pertain to a view of what is normative (e.g., the acceptance or rejection of God's law). Actually, types and time-currents go back to prephilosophical or religious commitments that had and still have a bearing on philosophical perspectives.

A More Detailed Explanation[3]

Taking a closer look at Vollenhoven's distinction between types and time-currents, we note that *the first main problem,* that of ontology, which philosophers—from the ancient Greeks (Tol 1993) to the twentieth-century commentators—and perhaps every human being at one time or another must answer, contains several questions.

The first of these concerns is becoming, or the origin of the world. Is the cosmos eternal, as Aristotle held, and becoming no more than a primarily determined unfolding? Is there perhaps a real process of becoming—a temporal cosmos filled with change formed by Plato's demiurge? Or, centuries later, by a limitless process, as is found in consistent evolutionism? Or is there a third alternative, as in mythical ways of thinking, in which one also believes in the generation of the deities, as in Gnosticism? (See p. 45 below.)

The second question asks whether the universe is originally a unity (monism) or a diversity (dualism). Spinoza, for instance, accepted a monistic viewpoint in which God and the world are one, while Aristotle distinguished between pure form—or God, the unmoved mover—and prime matter (see p. 39).

The third and fourth questions pertain especially to the anthropological standpoint (cf. pp. 49–55) and touch topics like whether there is an essential difference between humans and animals and whether humans are in principle nothing but matter.

---

2. See pages 30f.
3. This section anticipates topics that are discussed in Part Three. Those less familiar with Vollenhoven's work are advised to read Part Three first.

As one can readily see from these few examples, Vollenhoven was not interested in only one question, such as whether one must choose between dualism or monism. Rather, he was preoccupied with four—at times, five—philosophical questions that philosophers seek to answer by means of various categories. These questions have to do with ontology; with the hierarchy of humans and animals; and, in several conceptions, with their relationship to the world of the divine as well.

A philosopher like Spinoza, for instance, viewed the universe monistically, speaking as he did of "God or nature" (Lat. *deus sive natura*). Aristotle and the defenders of Aristotelianism, however, distinguished between an original duality: the unmoved mover, or God, and eternal matter. That is, matter is viewed cosmologically, not cosmogonically, or by way of becoming. In the philosophy of Spinoza, creative and created nature (Lat. *natura naturans* and *natura naturata*) logically and metaphysically merge and become one. Body and soul are like a clock with two faces, referring to two aspects—thinking and extension—that are basically the same. They concern two parallel modes of the same substance, which is God (Bril 1986, 134–36).

This diversity of main types is directly related to what Vollenhoven called "a diversity in the way of posing and answering problems" (1961c, 15). His method concerns an "ordering of all directions according to the answers given to the most important philosophical problems" (1950e, 11). It strives after an integral approach to the diversity of foundational problems, and it pursues a "Consequential Problem-historical Method" (Tol 1993, 2003a). As one actually investigates various philosophical conceptions, however, one often does not acquire all the needed information, working as one must at times with only a limited amount of given data (cf. p. 64). Naturally, such a "formidable" approach (Seerveld 1973, 127) demanded—and still demands—continual research and constant readiness to adjust its preliminary results, a demanding process Vollenhoven himself regularly implemented.

In addition to the first main problem, that of ontology (see Part Three), there looms incessantly *a second main problem*, that of the relationship between the ethical notions of good and evil, or *the place and the foundation of the divine law*. As we already observed, some Rationalistic philosophers appealed to human autonomy, while Irrationalistic thinkers denied the existence of any law, be it divine or human. In history—from the ancients to the postmodernists—there appears to be a continual change within the choice of one's position vis-à-vis the founding of criteria and norms (see Part Four).

4

As subsequent generations reread earlier answers, they altered, in a typological tradition, preceding viewpoints. To cite three examples: Pope Leo XIII (1879, his Encyclical *Aeterni Patris*) and twentieth-century neo-Thomists like Jacques Maritain partly altered the perspective of Thomas Aquinas, while John Dewey's positivistic-rationalistic Darwinism has been reworked into a form of pragmatism. And some current thinkers, notably the New-Age protagonists, have revived ancient Gnosticism (cf. O'Regan 2001). And so the *Zeitgeist* changes in a continual process of successive time-currents, and types are being "transformed" in a following time-current, as will be treated in Part Four below.

Vollenhoven's Own Standpoint[4]

Vollenhoven took a definite stand vis-à-vis the above-mentioned two main philosophical problems—ontology and the normative (see pp. 57f.). Here we shall summarize his position, concerning (1) the law, (2) creation, and (3) the law and creation together.

As for the Divine Law

Rationalists like Kant and post-Kantians claimed that humans are autonomous, being a law unto themselves; they are subject neither to a heteronomous nor to a theonomous law. During a later era, Ir-rationalist Nietzsche denied—and rightly so—such autonomous knowledge, but he also denied the existence of the divine law.

Vollenhoven distinguished between the created cosmos and the divine law that is valid for that which has been created. God created the cosmos with an internal structure, and he subjected the various functions of created beings to modal laws. Humans are especially commanded to love, as stated in Jesus's summary of the Decalogue: "You shall love the Lord your God ... [and] your neighbor as yourself" (Matthew 22:37–39). Within societal structures, the law must be "positivized," for instance, by the government of the state concerning its organization and in terms of marriage laws (1992, 127, 366). Vollenhoven summarized this point in his article "Cal-vinistische wijsbegeerte" (*OE*): "This law, the command to love, points directly to the human person, primarily to the heart." The core of his anthropology is found in "the distinction between inner and outer, understood in this sense that the first, the prefunctional heart, directs that which functions—in its relation to the law—toward good or evil."

---

4. This section is particularly concerned with the views of the law, which are discussed in Part Four. One could consider reading this section after first becoming acquainted with Part Four.

The modal laws pertain to humans in their societal connections and relationships to purely functional creatures: physical things, plants, and animals. "Being able to count well" expresses a modal law (the law for counting), in other words, for one dimension of what it means to be human—of the structure for being human. Counting or calculating—be it in support of Eichmann, one of Hitler's henchmen, or on behalf of the kingdom of God, according to God's image—expresses human direction (1992, 311). The biblical model for this distinction between structure and direction (cf. Wolters 1985, 49f., 72f.) is found in Psalm 1, which clearly contrasts the way of the "righteous" and the "wicked."

According to Vollenhoven, "God maintains his law, being the law giver; and those who display the image of God, image God to the extent that they observe the law as creature" (1992, 202). The concept of the image of God, for Vollenhoven, does not pertain to ontology but touches human direction—living in accord with God's commands (Bril 2000, 279). "Being the image of God . . . is in Scripture a feature of human life that humans can begin to lose by not living according to God's commands" (1992, 202; cf. Bril 2000, 278–80, regarding the image of God according to Vollenhoven, in distinction from Dooyeweerd's view).

Briefly put: Vollenhoven distinguished between structural laws, the love command, and positive laws formulated by office bearers with an eye to time and place. The latter provide societal regulation in a structured situation in the light of the commandment to love (cf. 1992, 105). One's response to this central command he called "direction."

Should one's attitude be positive and concur with this command, then one manifests the image of God. In other words, "the image of God" does not refer to the ontological structure of human beings; rather it concerns the desire to live or not to live according to God's command, choosing either the way of obedience or disobedience.

Concerning Creation

Scripture's first words are: "In the beginning God created the heavens and the earth" (Genesis 1:1). This perspective is irreconcilable with Aristotle's dualistic notion of the unmoved mover and eternal matter, as well as with a neo-Platonic monism, in which everything emanates through gradations from the One. It is also incompatible with Spinoza's monistic "God or nature." According to Vollenhoven, "Christianity is neither dualistic nor monistic" (1964a, 218).

Likewise, Vollenhoven avoided, as already mentioned, purely cosmological thinking and mythological thinking. A case of the latter is

Gnosticism, which holds that there are generations of deities and which shows an attitude of contempt toward the physical world, created as it is by an evil demiurge or creator god. Christians know that God created the world good: "God saw everything that he had made, and behold, it was very good" (Genesis 1:31). God reveals to young and old that they live in God's world.

Vollenhoven rejected the answers to the ontological questions about the structure of creation that we mentioned before.

Regarding God's Law and Divine Creation Together

The law of love—the "core" of Vollenhoven's anthropology, as we noted above—"points directly to the human person, primarily to the heart."

Since the law is the boundary between God and the cosmos, the law is also the boundary for scientific thinking (cf. Dooyeweerd 1953, 99). Human theoretical thought can grasp subjects as extensive as light years as well as much of creation, but it cannot comprehend God—the God of Abraham, Isaac, and Jacob. In fact, an ontology that analyzes God is not permitted, being neither possible nor necessary. As a matter of fact, theo-ontology—thinking with warrant about the nature of God, be it an Aristotelian dualism or Spinozistic monism—is beyond the pale. Ontology, which deals with "the vertical structure of things," applies to the structure of creation alone. For the Word of God "is a lamp to my feet and a light to my path" (Psalm 119:105). It is not there to blind us, as butterflies are when attracted by light, but to help us find our way in a world that belongs to God.

Calvin Seerveld, one of Vollenhoven's students, rightly entitled one of his publications "Biblical Wisdom underneath Vollenhoven's Categories for Philosophical Historiography" (1973). Such was, indeed, Vollenhoven's intention. He was devoted to—using words of Albert Wolters, another student of Vollenhoven—the "biblical basics for a reformational worldview" (1985).

B. VOLLENHOVEN: THE PERSON

After reviewing his problem-historical method, a brief biography of Dirk Hendrik Theodoor Vollenhoven is in order. More complete biographical information can be found in publications by Johan Stellingwerff (1992 and 2001).

Vollenhoven was born in Amsterdam in 1892. He studied theology as well as philosophy at the Free University (*Vrije Universiteit*) there, which was founded in 1880 by Abraham Kuyper. He successfully passed his comprehensive exams in both fields and received his doctorate in philosophy in 1918 upon submitting a striking thesis, *De wijsbegeerte der wiskunde van theïstisch standpunt* ("The Philosophy of Mathematics from a Theistic Standpoint"). This dissertation was unusual in bringing a theistic standpoint to bear upon the philosophy of mathematics. Compare, for example, the work of the eminent mathematicians Bertrand Russell and Alfred North Whitehead, who composed their three-volume work, *Principia Mathematica,* around the same time (1910–1913) with a view to demonstrating the intrinsically logical nature of mathematics in which a faith commitment is assumed to have no impact.

Vollenhoven then served in two pastorates, in Oost-Kapelle in the province of Zeeland (1918–1921) and in The Hague (1921–1926). In 1920, he took a study leave in Germany to study under Felix Krueger. Krueger was the successor of the famous psychologist Wilhelm Wundt, the "father of the Leipziger School." Both Wundt and Krueger were oriented to a form of parallelism (1956b, 38; 2000, 235).

Vollenhoven was appointed professor of philosophy at the Free University in 1926. Seven years later (1933), he published *Het Calvinisme en de Reformatie van de Wijsbegeerte* ("Calvinism and the Reformation of Philosophy"), in which he contrasted, on the one hand, the "basic themes of Scriptural philosophy," namely, the "direct sovereignty of God . . . over all things . . . and [the distinction] between God as Sovereign and that which he has created" (1933a, 23), with, on the other hand, the "basic themes of unscriptural philosophy in general," that is, their dualistic acceptance or monistic rejection of the law as the boundary between God and the cosmos (ibid., 51). The historical section begins with a brief overview of Greco-Roman thought and then traces how Christian thinking became mingled with pagan symbolism after the Gospel's entrance into the world—a commingling or synthesis that began to decrease in intensity after 1250. As its title, "Calvinism and the Reformation of Philosophy," already suggests, a Reformational approach to interpreting and evaluating philosophical issues is necessary.

In this development, Vollenhoven was compelled to distance himself from certain theses he had held earlier—first in his doctoral thesis (Tol 2003b) and then in his work of 1933. In 1950, Vollenhoven published Volume One of his *Geschiedenis der Wijsbegeerte* ("The History of Philosophy"). There he applies a revised method to the history of philosophy proper. In just less than 600 pages, Vollenhoven positions the Greek thinkers prior to Plato and Aristotle according to such main strands as universalism-individualism, mythical or nonmythical thinking, and views of the law (nonrealism before Plato).[5] Meanwhile, Vollenhoven outlined the larger flow of intellectual history in a "short survey of the history of philosophy" (1956b); in this manuscript of slightly over forty pages, the philosophies of Plato and Aristotle together occupy five pages of text.

He wrote, "The problem of the most important periods in the history of philosophy is closely connected with the history of the relationship between philosophy and Word-revelation" (1950e, 18). This takes into account that the Greeks and the Romans of the pre-Christian era did not know about the notions of God's creation of the universe as "good," creation of humanity in God's image, and the divine commandment of love—to love God and one's neighbor. In this connection, Vollenhoven explained the history of philosophical thinking according to three main divisions: first, pagan ways of thinking in antiquity (until c. A.D. 50); followed by a period of a *synthesis philosophy*, in which thinkers, especially the Scholastics, endeavored to combine the impressive structure of Platonic or Aristotelian thought with Christian motifs; and finally, after about 1450, the resistance to synthesis thinking by many Europeans, ushering in as they did antisynthetic thinking and an increasing secularization.[6]

C. VOLLENHOVEN AND DOOYEWEERD

Because Vollenhoven is often—and rightly so—named alongside of his brother-in-law, Herman Dooyeweerd (1894–1977),[7] we must briefly link the two Christian philosophers. Before they were both appointed professor at the Free University in 1926, they were already discussing issues facing the Christian faith and walk in both daily life and philosophy. These discussions took place while both were residents of The Hague, where Dooyeweerd worked at the Abraham Kuyper Stichting and Vollenhoven served as a pastor in a church.[8]

Shortly after the publication of Vollenhoven's "Calvinism and the Reformation of Philosophy," Dooyeweerd's major work appeared *De Wijsbegeerte der Wetsidee* ("Philosophy of the Cosmonomic Idea," 1933–

---

5. H. Evan Runner translated about half of this volume (Vollenhoven 1958a).
6. See p. 93f. below. The three division are clearly indicated in Vollenhoven 1950e, 18–19, but they are also already in 1933a.
7. See Henderson 1994; Verburg 1989; review Vunderink 1994, 221–26; cf. Stellingwerff 1992.
8. Cf. Vollenhoven, "Wijsbegeerte, Calvinistische," in *OE* xv, 586.

1935), so designated because the law (Gk. *nomos*) is seen as the boundary between God and the cosmos (Gk. *kosmos*).[9] Its English translation, *A New Critique of Theoretical Thought* (1953–1958), has a slightly different focus—it is a critique of Kant's pretended autonomy of human reason (cf. Yong Joon Choi 2000).

Both brothers-in-law were also deeply interested in the history of philosophy. Dooyeweerd's articles on Western intellectual thought, *Roots of Western Culture* (1979), a translation of his *Vernieuwing en Bezinning* (1959), sketched three historical periods—the Greco-Roman or pagan, the medieval, and the modern and contemporary or secular options (cf. Vunderink 1980, 268–73). As Dooyeweerd saw it, a person belongs to one of three traditions—pagan, secular, or Christian—implying that no one can develop a neutral or autonomous way of thinking.

When one compares Volume One of Vollenhoven's "History of Philosophy" with the first volume of Dooyeweerd's "Reformation and Scholasticism," one notices two distinct but "complimentary" approaches (Seerveld 1965, 200). Whereas Vollenhoven used four or five main categories or types, such as monism and dualism, Dooyeweerd interpreted the Greeks through a single basic polarity, that of matter and form. Similarly, whereas Vollenhoven used several main types and time-currents in capturing modern philosophy, Dooyeweerd worked only with one so-called basic ground motive, that of nature and freedom (*New Critique*, I, Part 2). On the other hand, there are also historiographic agreements (Bril 1995).

Some of their close associates prefer Vollenhoven's more detailed and complex method, while others are more in tune with Dooyeweerd's sole notion of ground motives (e.g., Vunderink 2000).

D. THE EFFECT ON REFORMATIONAL PHILOSOPHY

Students carried on the work of Vollenhoven's problem-historical method in Amsterdam; in Canada at the Institute for Christian Studies in Toronto and at Redeemer College; in the United States at Calvin College—H. Evan Runner, along with many of his students—and at Dordt College; in South Africa at Potchefstroom—J. Taljaart and his students—and at Bloemfontein; in Indonesia—Henk van der Laan; in Australia; and in New Zealand (cf. Bril 2000, 176–78).

---

9. As Dooyeweerd (1953–1958, 1:99) stated it: "In Christ the heart bows under the *lex* . . . as the *universal* boundary . . . between the *Being* of God and the *meaning* of His creation." (Cf. 4:132–33.)

The insights of both Vollenhoven and Dooyeweerd have had an even greater effect. The founders of Reformational philosophy, as they were called, played a crucial role in the formation of the Association of Calvinistic Philosophy in 1936 (later changed to the Association for Reformational Philosophy). Vollenhoven was president of the association until 1963, while Dooyeweerd was the editor-in-chief of the journal *Philosophia Reformata* from the association's inception in 1936 until his death in 1977.

Shortly after World War II, in the period 1948–1951, several chairs for Reformational philosophy were established at Dutch universities. Their first teachers were Sietse Zuidema (1906–1987) in Utrecht; Klaas J. Popma (1903–1986) in Utrecht and Groningen; Johan P. A. Mekkes (1898–1986) in Leiden; and Hendrik van Riessen (1911–2000) in Delft and later also in Eindhoven; with Jan Dengerink succeeding Popma in 1974. At present, there are six professors espousing a Reformationally informed philosophy at eight universities (not including the Free University in Amsterdam): Henk Geertsema in Groningen and Utrecht; Gerrit Glas in Leiden; Jan Hoogland in Twente; Roel Kuiper in Rotterdam; and, before his emeritus status, Egbert Schuurman in Delft, Eindhoven, and Wageningen; with Marc de Vries succeeding him in Delft and Maarten Verkerk in Eindhoven.

Fruits of the Reformational endeavors initiated by Vollenhoven and Dooyeweerd have been harvested at two recent international conferences hosted by the Association for Reformational Philosophy. The theme of the first one, which was actually the fifth international symposium held in 1994, was "Christian Philosophy at the Close of the Twentieth Century" (see Griffioen and Balk 1995).

The theme of the second symposium, held five years later in 2000, was "Cultures and Christianity A.D. 2000" (cf. "Proceedings," in *Philosophia Reformata* 66/1, 2001). Contributors came from five continents: from the United States, Richard J. Mouw, James W. Skillen, and Huai-Chen Chang; from Canada, Hendrik Hart; from the United Kingdom, Elaine Storkey; from Mexico, Adolfo García de la Sienra; from Argentina, Elsa R. de Powell; from South Africa, Elaine Botha, Daniel F. M. Strauss, and Bennie J. van der Walt; from Nigeria, Yusufu Turaki; from the Philippines, Melba Padilla Maggay; and Bong Ho Son from South Korea.

Kornelis A. Bril and Ralph W. Vunderink

EXPLORATIONS

Since Vollenhoven often expressed himself concisely and tersely, his method will be elucidated by means of historical examples. The choice of these examples, however, is mine. Vollenhoven's insights will also be compared with those of others who have traveled a similar path.

The plan is to make a number of exploratory journeys through the landscape of Western thought. Rather than trying to explain Vollenhoven's entire historical map, I will focus on some dimensions of his large map—sections of which he never got to—and clarify certain details that often prove difficult to comprehend at first sight or have been misjudged.

Part One highlights changing historical periods, including the internalizing or subjectivizing of the norms lying outside of, or behind, the cosmos, as Plato believed. Part Two reviews four models of historiography, namely those of Jan Hendrik van den Berg, Michel Foucault, Thomas Kuhn, and Vollenhoven. Then I explain Vollenhoven's distinctions between the so-called "types" or ontologies as different traditions of thought. Part Four gets at the question, "What must I do?" Philosophers over the course of time have answered this question differently and taken different positions regarding the pertinent norms and criteria. We will consider the place of religion and time-currents in this process.

Vollenhoven's labors in the problem-historical method can be helpful to those searching for answers for their own historical investigations. Those seeking to understand the background of the time and situation in which they live and who are seeking their own way may receive valuable insights from his work.

In closing, I wish to thank Anthony Tol from the Free University for his many helpful comments and John Kok of Dordt College Press for his careful editing of this English language publication.

K. A. B.

PART ONE

THE WORLD IN FRONT OF AND BEHIND THE EYE: FROM GALILEO TO POSITIVISM

I. A Rose in the Dutch Dunes

If one goes for a leisurely walk through the Dutch dunes on a given morning, one might find a rose—for instance, an eglantine or a sweet-briar. This flower has a reddish color; it is still somewhat wet on account of the morning dew; its flowers and leaves produce a lovely scent; and its leaves feel a bit colder than would those of an artificial rose.

The English philosopher John Locke would say that everything we just enumerated is altogether wrong. The rose's color and smell and the warmth or cold we feel upon touching it are so-called secondary qualities, which are found in the person perceiving the flower. The rose itself has only so-called primary qualities, like magnitude, form, motion, and extension—no secondary qualities. In his famous *An Essay Concerning Human Understanding*, Locke wrote that colors like violet and blue are "produced in our Minds" (II.viii.13) by the primary qualities residing in the external object: "Whiteness and Coldness are no more in Snow, than Pain is; yet those *Ideas* of Whiteness, and Coldness, Pain, *etc.* being in us the Effects of Powers in Things without us, ordained by our Maker to produce in us such Sensations; they are real *Ideas* in us, whereby we distinguish the Qualities, that are really in things themselves" (II.xxx.2).

Locke did not coin this common distinction; in fact, almost fifty years earlier, René Descartes wrote similarly in his *Principles of Philosophy*: "such sensations . . . as we call tastes, smells, sound, heat, cold, light, colors, etc., . . . in truth represent nothing to us outside of our mind" (1644, principle 71). In other words, grass is no longer green.

15

Vollenhoven and others believed that it was Galileo who first introduced this distinction in his *Il Saggiatore* (1623), translated as *The Assayer*.[1] In the conclusion of this work, the Italian astronomer wrote:

> I think that tastes, odors, colors, and so on are no more than mere names so far as the object in which we place them is concerned, and that they reside only in the consciousness. (ibid., 274)

That was the year in which a new era in the history of philosophy commenced, namely, that of early Rationalism or scientialism. That was the age of the great systems and the geometric gardens, in which René Descartes and Benedict Spinoza labored.

The green of the grass was no longer in the grass. Color became an internal subjective notion—in Locke's parlance, a secondary quality. For Vollenhoven, however, the reddish color of our rose is one of many external "object functions" of the rose.[2] To Locke, its color is only an idea within us.

This process of subjectification, which started in Rationalism, continued in the following period, in the ages of rococo and pre-Romanticism. In philosophy, this was the age of the Enlightenment.

Johann George Sulzer (1720–1779), a leading adherent of the Romantic garden type,[3] held that the origin of our feelings is not found in something or someone around us; rather, the origin of our feelings is found solely and wholly within ourselves. After the death of his wife, he wrote: "This loss had amazingly affected me" (G. *Dieser Verlust hat mich erstaundlich angegriffen*). He wrote "amazingly"; he was astonished that his feelings originated within himself, that is, that they were subjective.

As time went on, the distance between the internal and the external[4] increased. According to Jan van den Berg, the gap between humans and their world grew larger. As the rose ceased to be a flower, similarly "wa-

---

1. For the English translation of *The Assayer*, see Drake 1957, 229–80.
2. Vollenhoven 1967b, §64; for the context in which he explains this point cf. p. 75f. below.
3. As cited by Van den Berg (1961, 186).
4. The terms *internal* and *external* are borrowed from Van den Berg. In his best-known book, *The Changing Nature of Man* (1961) or *Metabletica* (from Gk. *metablētikos, metabolē* "exchange") (in Dutch in 1956), Van den Berg, a professor at the University of Leiden, treats the theory of change in the history of culture and of the mind. Vollenhoven and Van den Berg never referred to each other in their respective writings and possibly never read each other's works. Both, however, were fascinated by the appearance of historical periods and by the process of interiorization taking place therein.

ter became H_2O," thereby "losing an element."[5] The external world became numb and soulless.

At the same time, feelings lost their object: they became "thingless feelings," said Johann N. Tetens, Immanuel Kant, and Johann G. Fichte.[6] For Anthony Shaftesbury (1671–1713), inner experience determined the norm, *inward* being his "favorite adjective."[7] And Sir William Hamilton (1788–1856) wrote that, regarding the object of one's feeling, there is "nothing but what is subjectively subjective, there is no object different from self."[8] The origin of our feelings is to be located within us.

A corresponding development can be traced in the history of spirituality. Faith became more and more internalized; in Roman Catholicism it appeared as a quietism,[9] while in Protestantism it surfaced as pietism.[10] Angelus Silesius (1624–1677) wrote, "Even if Christ were born a thousand times over in Bethlehem, but not in your soul, you would yet be lost."[11] And, he added, "The cross at Golgotha does not deliver you from the weight of guilt, unless it be erected also within you."

There is a noteworthy parallel in the history of the Jewish Kabbala. In his spiritualistic exercises, the earlier "Merkaba rider" sets out for the throne carriage, the Merkaba, of God. In Hasidim, a later form of Kabbala, according to Gershom Scholem,

> It is by descending into the depths of his own self that man wanders through all the dimensions of the world; in his own self he lifts the barriers which separate one sphere from the other; in his own self, finally, he transcends the

5. Van den Berg (1961, 24) refers to the four ancient elements—earth, water, air, and fire—which the Greeks associated with the farmer, the fisherman, the miller, and the blacksmith. See further Van den Berg 1977, 128–31.

   Translator's note: By reducing water to H_2O, that is, to its physical chemical aspect, water is no longer seen as a way of irrigating growing crops, as a possibly deadly threat during a hurricane, as a thirst quencher in a desert, as a means of baptizing believers, or as a lovely lake, for instance. As Van den Beukel, a physicist at the Technical University in Delft, put it: "'In that case,' one might ask, 'is water not H_2O?' No, water is not H_2O. At most it is also H_2O. H_2O is one aspect of water-ness" (1991, 52).

6. Van den Berg 1961, 188.

7. As Jan Romein reminds us (1971, 439).

8. Van den Berg, ibid.

9. Cf. Van den Berg 1968, 206–85: "The fifth period of the inner . . . from 1540 to 1740. The absolute interiorized faith. . . ."

10. Pietism also opposes the "reasonable religion" of the old liberals, who short-changed feelings (cf. p. 77f. below).

11. Angelus Silesius, a pseudonym of Johannes Scheffler, who wrote *The Celestial Drifter*, changed from Lutheranism to Roman Catholicism (1653).

17

limits of natural existence and . . . discovers that God is "all in all" and there is "nothing but Him." (1954, 341)

In both Protestant pietism and the Jewish Kabbala, then, faith became internalized. Even if there were no direct influence of the one upon the other, there is what Van den Berg would call a "metabletic connection" (cf. p. 23 below).

The shift from the external to the internal reached the Low Countries somewhat later. In his study about the history of religious liberalism, specifically of the theological Groningen School and its leader Hofstede de Groot, Karel Roessingh wrote, "The Groningers were very resolute in finding . . . the essence of religion to reside in feeling" (1926 i, 31), and cites Hofstede de Groot's words: "Unshakable and certain is only that which rests on the personal conviction of the heart, on one's emotional life, on inner experience" (ibid.).

Thus faith can be described as a process of internalizing, interiorizing, subjectifying, or a priorizing (see Figure 1 and Part Four).

II. Assessments of the Process of Interiorization

We described a part of the history of the internal-external relationship, a process Van den Berg characterized as an "ill-fated separation" between unsensing things and thingless feelings (1956, 249). Others, insofar as they noticed such a change, gave their own interpretation of it. The German philosopher Heinz Heimsoeth (1886–1975), for instance, devoted the third of his "six great themes of Western metaphysics" to the theme of "Soul and External World." He observed a process of interiorization, as did Van den Berg. Going back to earlier centuries, he cited Johannes Kepler (1571–1630), who described the soul as "freed . . . from all the objectivizing onus," and René Descartes, who described it as "free from any essential link with [the] external world." It was Leibniz who considered the soul as "closed up within itself in its pure inwardness for all time," that is, as "the totality of ideas . . . drawn into the soul."[12] Though Heimsoeth was preoccupied with the same process of internalization as were Van den Berg and Vollenhoven, he applauded what Van den Berg deplored.

---

12. Heimsoeth 1994, 131 (Kepler), 132 (Descartes), and 136–37 (Leibniz).

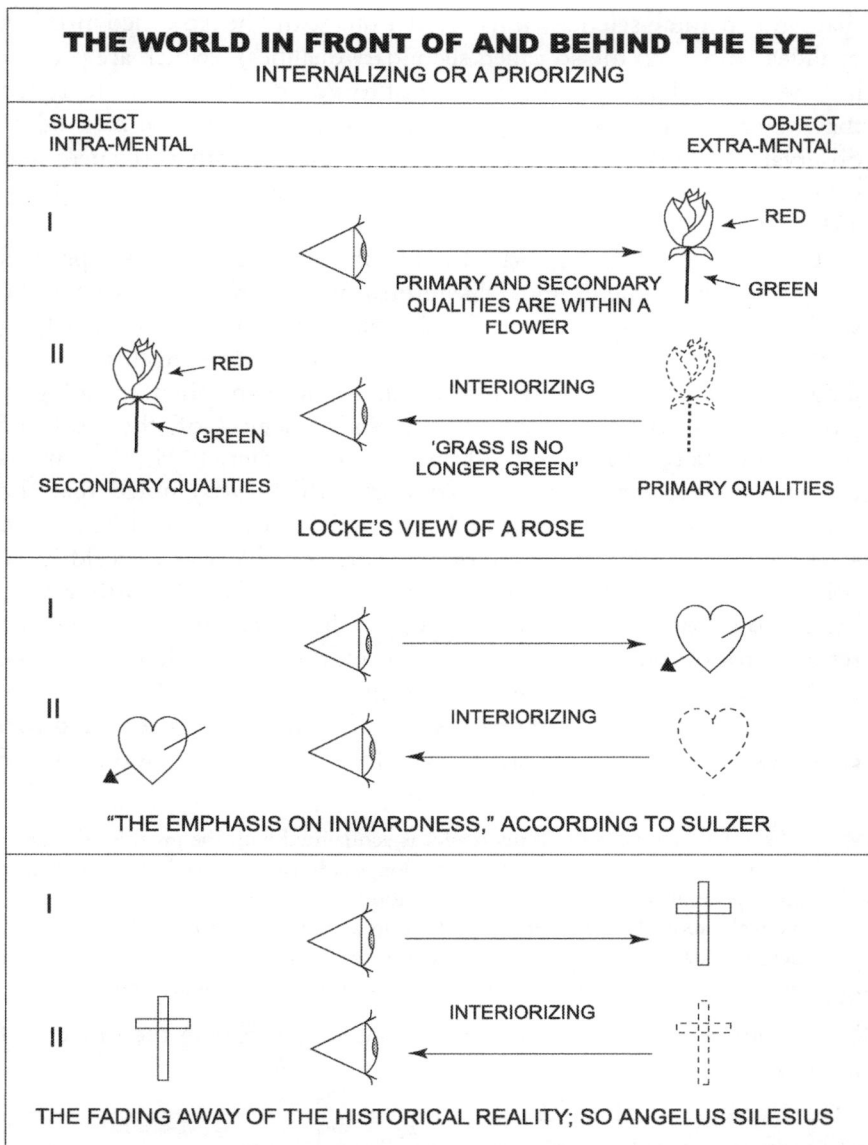

THE WORLD IN FRONT OF AND BEHIND THE EYE
INTERNALIZING OR A PRIORIZING

SUBJECT
INTRA-MENTAL

OBJECT
EXTRA-MENTAL

I — RED

PRIMARY AND SECONDARY
QUALITIES ARE WITHIN A
FLOWER

GREEN

II — RED

INTERIORIZING

GREEN

'GRASS IS NO
LONGER GREEN'

SECONDARY QUALITIES

PRIMARY QUALITIES

LOCKE'S VIEW OF A ROSE

I

II

INTERIORIZING

"THE EMPHASIS ON INWARDNESS," ACCORDING TO SULZER

I

INTERIORIZING

II

THE FADING AWAY OF THE HISTORICAL REALITY; SO ANGELUS SILESIUS

Figure 1: Schematic summary of three historical examples of the theme of a priorizing

Whereas Heimsoeth dealt with the history of the internal, Dijkster-huis described the history of the external. In *The Mechanization of the World Picture,* he observes that Plato's ideas have become a priorized and that Galileo coined the notion of secondary qualities. He further noted

19

that "the natural sciences must deal only with the so-called primary qualities" (not with the so-called secondary qualities),[13] which are present in "the mind" (Lat. *in mente*). In contrast to Van den Berg, who regretted that water "became" H_2O, for Dijksterhuis, this mechanical method of observation implied a stimulating program for the natural sciences and ushered in a healthy development for the science of physics (1961, 431f.).

Unlike Heimsoeth, who saw the history of the internal as a process of spiritual enrichment, and Dijksterhuis, who viewed the mechanistic worldview as an improvement for the cause of physics, Van den Berg deplored these two developments. But he was not alone in this negative judgment. In 1935, Edmund Husserl, a German phenomenologist, pointed out a common disregard for, and a neglect of, the world of one's daily life (G. *Lebenswelt*)[14]; about a decade earlier (1924), the American philosopher Sir Edwin Arnold Burtt (1892–1989) noted that the "gloriously romantic universe of Dante and Milton . . . had now been swept away. . . . The really important world outside was a world hard, cold, colourless, silent, and dead."[15] And in 1925, Alfred North Whitehead wrote ironically that "nature gets credit which should in truth be reserved for ourselves; the rose for its scent: the nightingale for his song. . . . Nature is a dull affair, soundless, scentless, colourless."[16]

A similar critique of the process of interiorization was rendered two centuries earlier by the English essayist Joseph Addison,[17] who launched an ironic protest in the *Spectator* (1712):

> I have here supposed that my reader is acquainted with the great modern discovery. . . [which at that time, but no longer afterward, people experienced as an important news item]: Light and colours . . . are only ideas in the mind . . . we walk about like the enchanted hero in a romance, who sees beautiful castles, woods and meadows . . . but the fantastic scene breaks up, and the desolate knight finds himself on a barren heath, or in a solitary desert.

Thus, Van den Berg is by no means alone in bemoaning the process of interiorization.[18]

---

13. See below, p. 70; and Dijksterhuis and Forbes 1961, i, 163.
14. Husserl 1954, 142, 224. Apart from this point, Husserl maintained this position even after his turn toward Idealism, whereby he attempted to maintain the notion of normativeness and thus culture (so De Boer 1966, 568–74, 600; cf. 570: "Consciousness is not nature, but nature constitutes itself in consciousness").
15. Burtt 1924, 238–39 (cf. *Dictionary of the History of Ideas* iii, 397 concerning Newton).
16. Whitehead 1925 (end of chapter 3).
17. *Dictionary of the History of Ideas* iii, 398.

What happened after 1900? At the turn of the century, a fundamental turning point took place[19] as the enchantment with interiorization began to wane. Bertrand Russell, after a brief flirtation with Hegelianism (1894–1898) and Idealism, was relieved that he could conclude again that grass was actually green—it was like an escape from prison.[20] The beautiful things we see in creation really are beautiful. In Genesis 1:11–12 (NIV), we read: "Then God said, 'Let the land produce vegetation: seed-bearing plants and trees on the land that bear fruit with seed in it. . . .' And God saw that it was good."

Evaluating our first exploratory journey, we conclude that there are periods of predominant "time-currents," as Vollenhoven named them, which orient the thought of a period. These Western thought structures change from time to time; they do not remain constant. Further, history does not appear to be a gallery filled with statues without any connection to each other. But one of the central problems in this process—of change and connection—appears to be how the external and the internal are related: the a priorizing and interiorizing of the secondary qualities, as well as the internalizing in other fields,[21] such as physics, psychology, and the realm of faith. After this, our first exploratory journey, I will turn to a number of Vollenhoven's seemingly "unintelligible" texts that inspired me to make this journey.[22] It may very well be that after reading my explanation, these texts will no longer be as incomprehensible as they at first appeared, though they do remain extremely brief. The reader may also compare my travel account with Vollenhoven's own "maps and charts."[23]

Thus far, we have been concerned with successive eras, in which a remarkable measure of synchronic unity existed between various intellectual fields within a given historical period. This has been our first journey into history. Next, for our second journey, we shall view this synchronic unity in connection with a diachronic approach of history.

---

18 Cf. Bril 1986, 230–37.

19. In Part Four, we will return to this theme of historical episodes in the theme of a priori.

20. "With a sense of escaping from prison, we allowed ourselves to think that grass is green, that the sun and stars would exist if no one was aware of them," confessed Bertrand Russell (1951, 12).

21. This is the connection between the external and the internal for which Van den Berg was looking when he spoke of the *medium* (cf. Bril 1986, 20, 22–23, 236).

22. Vollenhoven devotes no fewer than ten lines to Galileo and his notion of secondary qualities in 1956 (1956b, 33; cf. p. 75 below) and four lines to him in 1959 (1959a, 40), but he omits Galileo in his summary article (1964a).

23. Translator's note: Klaas Popma, one of Vollenhoven's close associates, typified his labors as mapmaking and Vollenhoven himself as a cartographer (1941, 50).

PART TWO

TYPES AND TIME-CURRENTS

In this part, I shall discuss four models of historiography—those of the Dutchman Jan Hendrik van den Berg, the Frenchman Michel Foucault, the American Thomas Kuhn, and Vollenhoven—to be followed by a further orientation in the last model. We shall compare Vollenhoven's problem-historical method with those of the other three authors, as well as treat their terminology "from the outside"; in Parts Three and Four, we shall treat them more "from the inside."

I. Four Models of Historiography

One can describe the history of a culture and the history of philosophy in different ways, as the following four models will show.

A. GOING THROUGH TIME IN "CLOSED RANKS"

We commence with our first model, that of Van den Berg.[1] Within the history of a culture, such as the architecture of church buildings, one can see the periods of the basilica, the Romanesque, the Gothic, the Renaissance, and the Baroque styles, each of which has its own character. In addition to architecture, this cultural unity manifests itself in various other areas of a certain era: not only in the natural sciences, medicine, and literature but also in mysticism and spirituality. That is, every epoch has its own lifestyle. Seemingly greatly differing facts from the same period appear nevertheless to be related (synchronism), or, as Van den Berg put it, "That synchronic facts cohere (within one cultural area), that is a metabletical law," and there is "the method of synchronic facts" (1984, 100, 198). Successively, Van den Berg sketched periods within which a far-reaching

---

1. Cf. Parabirsing 1974; Peeters 1978; Bril 1986; Ouweneel 1991, and Zwart 2002.

measure of concurring developments exists between the most divergent areas of human life: from physiology to the devotion to Mary, from mathematics to the art of painting, and from transportation to mysticism. Everything, according to Van den Berg, "marches through time in closed ranks" (1977, 201; see also 1968, 384). Our first model touches primarily a synchronic historiography ("closed ranks," the horizontal line).

In addition, Van den Berg analysed themes between historical periods—diachronic historiography (the vertical line) within distinct areas, such as the histories of anatomy and of spirituality—which, as he saw it, in every way confirm synchronism. If one combines the horizontal and the vertical lines, one can accept Struyker Boudier's designation of diasynchronism (1975), though the essence of metabletica is found in synchronology.

Metabletica, a theory about change, receives its relief precisely when one focuses on the "changes" between successive but discontinuous periods.[2] Concerning this method of historiography, Willem Ouweneel wrote, "In this respect, metabletica, as far as I can check, may be called truly unique" (1991, 245). To see if his claim is correct, permit me to compare his view with the second historiographic model, that of the twentieth-century French philosopher Michel Foucault, who died in 1984.

B. A STRUCTURAL VISION: ANONYMOUS THINKING

We limit Foucault's historiographic view to his book translated as *The Order of Things*. Foucault (1926–1984), like Van den Berg, distinguished between historical periods, such as those of the Renaissance (c. 1500–1600), of the classics (c. 1600–1800), and of the modern period of the last two centuries (c. 1800–2000). Every period has its own structure, an unnamed order, whose foundation he called *episteme*, or knowledge ("the epistemological field"). The depth of the *episteme* of a certain epoch determines that human speech, perception,[3] acting, and thinking are superficial phenomena, that they are phenomena of what is actually an unidentified

---

2. Tabular surveys of periods are found in Parabirsing, 116f.; Peeters, 174–77; and Van den Berg 1968, 142; 1973, 166 (cf. Bril 1986, 294).

3. Foucault (1970) claimed that in the Renaissance, perception differed from that of the classical time of Descartes and others (cf. Bakker 1973, 67, 71) (a difference we also noticed concerning the interpretation of the rose [in Part One]). In his subsection on order (in the chapter on representing), Foucault stated that the "age of resemblance [the sixteenth century] is drawing to a close" and that Descartes (as well as Bacon) "rejects resemblance" and "universalizes" the act of comparison" (1970, 51–52). For Foucault's further specific views in this context, we refer the reader to Bakker and Merquior (1985).

thinking. *Episteme* simultaneously decentralizes the subject, creating the opposite of autonomous humanism. Socioeconomic aspects are themselves determined by the *episteme;* they do not determine human thinking. It took a measure of courage to proclaim this truth in Paris, where at that time (1966) Marxism occupied a dominant position in the academic world.

In each of the three above-mentioned periods, Foucault treated three areas: human language, natural history, and economics. "[The] naturalists, economists, and the grammarians employed the same rules," he wrote, "to define the objects proper to their own study, to form their concepts, and to build their theories" (1970, xi). He, in turn, "tried to determine the basis or archaeological system common to an whole series of scientific 'representations' or 'products' dispersed throughout the natural history, economics, and philosophy of the Classical period" (ibid., xi–xii). These sharply delineated periods, according to Foucault, appear to be mutually discontinuous, separated as they are by a sharp caesura. For there are no gradual transitions from the one period to the other; there are only mutations.[4]

Comparing Van den Berg and Foucault

Before discussing our third model, I shall first compare the models of Van den Berg and Foucault. Everyone who reads their works cannot but be struck by a certain degree of mutual agreement. At least three commentators have noted a similarity between Foucault's concept of *episteme* and Van den Berg's notion of a metabletical period.[5] There is a strong measure of "homogeneity" (G. *Einheitlichkeit*) within a period (holism rather than pluralism), and, according to both authors, there is also a significant difference between periods.[6]

Foucault and Van den Berg differ, however, regarding where the periods fall. Foucault distinguished only three periods between the pre-Renaissance and today, while Van den Berg listed about ten periods between 1429 and the present. Van den Berg's unique feature is that he closely linked the changes to certain dates, such as 1543, the year of Copernicus and of the great anatomist Vesalius (1968, 314–19). This is not

---

4. It appears that the later Foucault no longer kept all of his earlier theses (Lambrechts 1982, 31; Bril 1986, 16).
5. Parabirsing, 238–45; Struyker Boudier, 56–61; and Peeters, 167ff.
6. Gaston Bachelard (1884–1962) had brought ideas about differences between periods to the table. He influenced Georges Canguilhem (1904–1995) and together they influenced Michel Foucault (1985, 31). Van den Berg became acquainted with the same structure of thought (Parabirsing, 241–44).

a coincidence but a "metabletical necessity" for him. Many other examples can be found in his works that have been published since 1959.

Foucault's thought is related to structuralism, that of Van den Berg to phenomenology (especially to his early work of an existentialist nature). Unlike Van den Berg, Foucault is akin to Nietzsche.[7]

By way of a final, remarkable difference, Van den Berg, at least, prior to the coming of a new period, signaled the large influence of the individual. He wrote:

> Historical personages *act*, they are not propelled. The course of events is in the hands of a few daring individuals. History is the history of the *great*, of those taking on big decisions and simultaneously assuming great responsibilities. (1956, 250)[8]

Van den Berg sailed altogether different waters from those of Foucault, who emphasized anonymity: individuals, like a he or a she, do not make a claim. Mere words are being spoken. This is apparent already from the opening paragraph of his inaugural address (1970), which reads (in translation): "At the moment of speaking, I would like to have perceived a nameless voice, long preceding me." This difference between our two authors is related to the already signaled difference between existentialism and structuralism.[9]

The Two Models and Their Problems

Because Foucault and Van den Berg cannot both be right in their historical periodization, there is clearly a question concerning a sound criterion for the nature of a historical period. Van den Berg—in my opinion correctly—pointed to a transition circa 1900, a claim that Foucault denied. The Dutch historian Jan Romein also refers to "a divisive gap" between the nineteenth and twentieth centuries in the Western world (1967). Vollenhoven and many others likewise ascertain a radical

---

7. Foucault's ideas have been typified as neo-anarchistic (Merquior, 155–160), a designation that Van den Berg, especially in his extensive study *Hooligans* (1989), fiercely opposed.
   Concerning the link between Foucault and Nietzsche, Trombadori remarked: "Nietzsche remains his most important theoretical point of reference" (1985, 99); D. J. Bos wrote: "Foucault himself says to have been influenced greatly by Nietzsche, notably as far as his views of truth and power are concerned" (1985, 87). The subject of "Nietzsche and Truth" is discussed below (cf. p. 87f.).
8. Cf. Ouweneel, 222–23.
9. In contrast to Van den Berg, Foucault misjudged freedom and responsibility (cf. Griffioen 1990, 59).

philosophical transition around 1900, namely, the transition from Rationalism to Irrationalism.

I object to the interpretation that both Foucault and Van den Berg put an inordinate emphasis on the unity between persons living at about the same time—the holistic interpretation. For example, Charles Darwin agreed to some extent, and yet disagreed strongly, with Jean-Baptiste Lamarck and Ernst Haeckel. Speaking on behalf of a number of biologists at the beginning of the nineteenth century, K. Figlio mentioned a "striking unity" and an "equally striking discord" (1976, 32), a "unity which underlay the apparent diversity of opinion" between them.

Finally, I object (an essential objection for our further argumentation) to the extreme discontinuity said to be between periods. For there are also traditions cutting through various periods. For instance, the materialistic tradition—to which Democritus belonged centuries ago and which appealed to the French molecular biologist Jacques Monod as well as the mythological tradition of second-century Gnosticism—influences even today's thinking (Quispel 1988; Van Wersch 1990; O'Regan 2001). We can also point to the effect of the Thomistic tradition in the Roman Catholic world and the continuous influence of Spinozism. Vollenhoven called such mental traditions "types."

C. THE THIRD HISTORIOGRAPHIC MODEL: THOMAS KUHN

Paradigms and Scientific Revolutions

Compared with Foucault's *episteme,* Thomas Kuhn's[10] concept of a paradigm has often been misinterpreted. To compare both concepts, also in connection with our fourth model, we shall first illustrate Kuhn's theory by means of two examples.

First, the Copernican revolution is a well-known astronomical revolution, which replaced the earlier prevailing Ptolemaic worldview. In the Ptolemaic worldview, all heavenly bodies move in circular orbits around the earth, but the planets describe a second circular orbit on a basic orbit, an epicycle.[11] For more than 1300 years, this Ptolemaic model was used to calculate rather carefully the location of the planets.

---

10. An introduction to Kuhn as a person and his place in the philosophy of science is found in Koningsveld (1976) (cf. Bril 1986, 25–35). Here we treat only parts of his philosophy in the framework of the problematics of our subject.

11. For example, should the planet Jupiter one year be found in the constellation of the Gemini, a year later it may appear much more to the left, namely, in the constellation of Virgo. One can measure this distance, which is about thirty degrees per year, with the

27

Based on developments in astronomy from Nicolas Copernicus to Isaac Newton, the new worldview placed the sun, not the earth, at the center; the new theory, likewise, explained the same movements of the planets (the so-called wandering stars) in the firmament.[12] Due to a scientific turnabout, the old paradigm (the standard theory), according to Kuhn, was replaced by a completely new theory. But the new paradigm had to be able to explain the astronomical phenomena and their problems better than did the old theory.

We speak of a "Copernican revolution," as did Kuhn, who attributes tde above-mentioned scientific revolution to Copernicus (1970, 117). But this designation contradicts Kuhn's own principle, for, according to him, one can speak of a new paradigm only when it receives at least wide recognition within a discipline, so that a new "disciplinary matrix" can be coined. But according to the historian of science I. Bernhard Cohen, the "Copernican revolution," about which historians have written so extensively, never took place. The first seventy years after its publication in 1543, Copernicus's book hardly exercised any influence. Not before circa 1610, with the appearance of Johannes Kepler's *Astronomia Nova,* did a truly astronomical revolution take place, a revolution that, as Cohen explains, can no longer really be labeled "Copernican."[13] As I see it, Cohen also correctly views the radical change proposed by Darwin as a remarkable "Darwinian revolution" (1985, 283–300).

A second historical example of a paradigm shift, according to Kuhn, is the theory of combustion. In earlier centuries, scientists did not say that combustion was oxidation (of wood or coal, e.g.) by oxygen, but they did note that many things, such as wood and coal, become lighter when burned. They then reasoned that something like phlogiston (a principle of fire) was being removed. Lavoisier is credited with being the author of the scientific revolution with his "oxygen theory of combus-

---

palm of one's outstretched hand. Should one look carefully, however, it appears that during a number of days this planet (and other planets) moves a few degrees to the right, thus making a loop or epicycle.

12. In Spoelstra's 1979 study one finds clear illustrations of the movement of "wandering stars" (planets, "looping") in the firmament (79) and of Ptolemy's classical explanatory model (83); also the explanation according to the new model of Johannes Kepler and others (118). Cf. Dijksterhuis 1961; and Bynum 1981, 80–81, 348–52.

13. Cohen (1985) and his interview in *NRC-Handelsblad* July 3, 1990.

Translator's note: In *The Copernican Revolution* (1957), Thomas Kuhn wrote more carefully: "The Copernican astronomical system . . . is, therefore, a joint product of Kepler and Copernicus" (212; and "one of the outstanding representatives [of the new climate of scientific thought] is Copernicus" ibid, 209).

tion."[14] (As an aside, he himself became the victim of another revolution; the tribunal judged that "the revolution does not need scholars" and had him executed by means of the guillotine.)

Epistemic and Paradigmatic Differences

Many authors consider Kuhn's theory of paradigms to be more or less identical to Foucault's notion of *episteme* (Merquior 1985, 36–38; and the Swiss psychologist Jean Piaget). Some, like Parabirsing, compared Kuhn's paradigms with Van den Berg's metabletical periods.

These concepts, it is true, aim to indicate a discontinuity between the preceding and succeeding phases. But it is incorrect to typify Kuhn's view, as did Parabirsing, for instance, as "In every cultural period people think differently" (1974, 225). For Foucault and Van den Berg concerned themselves with synchronic periods, with timeframes that, nevertheless, show a great unity in diverging areas. Kuhn was interested in vertical lines, in diachrony, in historical developments which for the separate sciences. In addition to the two paradigms mentioned above, Kuhn referred to other paradigms, to those of the Aristotelian and the Newtonian dynamics, respectively, as well as to corpuscular and wave optics. It appears that for Kuhn, the several paradigm switches (revolutions) never coincide in one historical period.

Further, a paradigm, according to Kuhn, can be shared only by a small "scientific community" within a subsection of a special science (1977, 294–96), as a bacteriophage group that has a hundred or merely ten or twenty members—a contrast to *episteme,* which, as Foucault sees it, includes all members.

Van den Berg and Foucault looked for the *synchronic unity* in a period. When Van den Berg viewed history diachronically, for instance, looking at the history of anatomy, architecture, and spirituality, he emphasized the mutual unity in a period, the "closed ranks" of an era. In contrast, Kuhn viewed the *separate diachronic developments* (per a disciplinary matrix[15]). Werner Diederich, who compiled a reader including Kuhn and his dis-

---

14. Kuhn 1970, 69; cf. 56, 118; cf. Van Nieuwenburg 1961, 86, 89, and 102. It took some time before the new oxygen theory was accepted—in Germany twenty years later than in France (Van Nieuwenburg). For the rest, the period, during which light was viewed sometimes as a wave and sometimes as a particle, lasted still many years more (Kuhn 1970, 114; 1972, 13–16). The concept of "scientific revolution" is here less suitable.
15. Regarding a scientific discipline, Thomas Kuhn also spoke later of a "disciplinary matrix" (instead of a paradigm).

cussion partners, rightly added the subtitle, "Contributions to a Diachronic Theory of Science" (1974).

Paradigms and the History of Philosophy

Most of Kuhn's examples of paradigmatic developments pertain to the history of the special sciences; he also spoke of "metaphysical paradigms" (1970, 184) and of paradigms with a communal ontology ("shared commitments . . . in the community's work," [1977, 298]). This approach has been applied to the history of philosophy (De Rijk 1977) as metaparadigms (Van Hoorn 1972). One could point to vitalistic paradigms, which throughout the centuries sustained several transformations, from the Thomistic paradigm (from Thomas Aquinas to neo-Thomism), to metaphysical materialism (from Democritus to Monod's molecular biology), and to a dualistic paradigm (from Plato, via Descartes, to the neurologist John Eccles).[16]

D. THE FOURTH MODEL: THE PROBLEM-HISTORICAL METHOD

Our first two models (those of metabletic periods and of completely discontinuous *epistemes* of anonymous human beings) are both synchronic in nature; Kuhn's paradigms are diachronic in character. We can compare these three models with a fourth model, that of Vollenhoven, who combined horizontal time-currents and vertical types or mental traditions in the history of human thought—diasynchrony.[17]

When it comes to philosophical research, one deals primarily with philosophical systems, or conceptions, composed by other philosophers. But in these conceptions, we can distinguish both the diachronic and synchronic moments. The elementary principle of this method is as follows: every philosopher is influenced by his contemporaries and by his predecessors, while he in turn can influence his contemporaries and those who come later. Hank Hart captured this method concisely in his dissertation (1966, xii):

---

16. There is no unanimity among several philosophical disciplines, which amounts to a *polyparadigmatic* situation. Kuhn emphasized that in a mature science, unanimity prevails concerning the foundational lines of a theory (monoparadigmatic perspective). But several authors either deny or refute this claim (e.g., Popper and Agassi [1973, 625; 1975, 320, 495] for physics).

17. Concerning this term, in a not entirely identical context, compare Parabirsing and Struyker Boudier.

The procedure roughly goes as follows. Through the study of the history of philosophy one tries to detect which problem-patterns of a general character go together. If one has found a large number of such patterns and has seen the way in which these are related, the most important thing is to find out if a particular conception actually falls into one of the patterns found so far. After a very long and tedious process a general-comparative framework of conception structures starts to emerge somewhat as follows.

	Type A	Type B	Type C
scientific Rationalism	Hobbes		
Positivism	Darwin		
Pragmatism	Dewey	James	Pierce

This small-scale model is oversimplified, but it gives an example of what is intended. Working with this method always means trying to find for every philosophical conception its "type-line" and its "period-line" in order to place it in a position of systematic comparison. This work greatly facilitates finding the conceptual framework within which a philosopher usually works.

According to Hart's schematic reproduction of Vollenhoven's model, the pragmatist John Dewey belongs to the same type as his predecessors Thomas Hobbes and Charles Darwin, while the pragmatists William James and Charles Peirce, though they participate in the same time-current as Dewey, are partly his spiritual kinsmen, partly his opposites.

Arend van Dam's caricature clarifies our point. As Dewey is writing, he is conscious of a tension between himself and his opponents of a similar mentality who adhere to other typological traditions (see Figure 2).

Figure 2: The influence on an author by his contemporaries

31

II. THE PROBLEM-HISTORICAL METHOD: A FURTHER ORIENTATION

Hart's chart, on the previous page, suggests an agreement between Thomas Hobbes, Charles Darwin, and John Dewey; for one thing, Dewey often referred to Darwin's evolutionistic view. It is also clear that, on many points, the three pragmatists mentioned both agreed and considerably disagreed with one another. Using Wittgenstein's term *family resemblance,* one could say that every element may be different and yet the same. G. E. Lock (1981) succeeded to clarify the term *family resemblance* with a drawing (Figure 3).

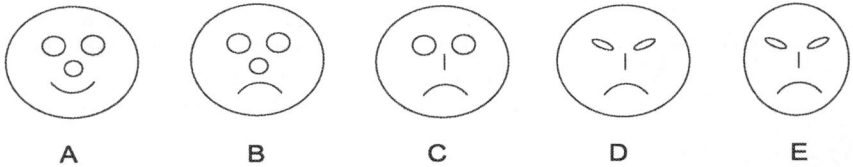

Figure 3 Family resemblances

"As one can see, the faces of A and E do not have a common aspect, but they are connected through a group of family resemblances going from A to E, via B, C, and D" (1981, 47).

Employing the above principle, we shall try to visualize Vollenhoven's method (Figure 4). We have taken three vertical types, or traditions of thought, to be compared with "metaphysical paradigms" and a number of horizontal time-currents that are comparable with the earlier-cited metabletical periods, or *epistemes.*

A. FOUR TIME-CURRENTS

The first time-current mentioned in Figure 4 goes back to the beginning of early Rationalism, namely, to scientialism. It was the time of the great philosophical systems (Fr. *l'esprit de système*), those of René Descartes, Benedict Spinoza, Thomas Hobbes, and Gottfried Wilhelm von Leibniz. These thinkers were "hard workers, frequently bachelors," with little patience for "emotional hearts," who were filled with an ardent commitment "to be reasonable" (cf., Heyden1968, 1969).

The Enlightenment, which Van den Berg labeled pre-Romanticism (1984, 167), came next. This was an age marked not by the geometric gardens of Descartes and Spinoza, but by the romantic ones of Voltaire, Jean Jacques Rousseau, and Denis Diderot. Let me characterize the common thread in Diderot and his two anonymous Enlightenment representatives, also portrayed in Figure 4,[18] in a not-too-responsible manner, as the "grin of Voltaire."

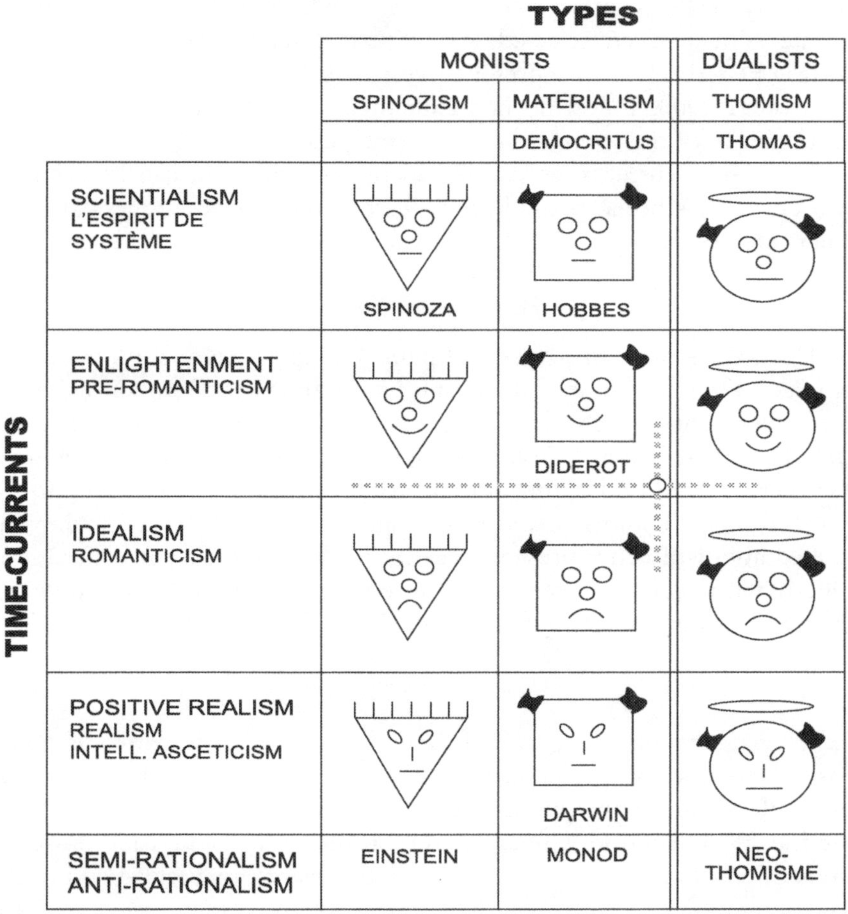

Figure 4: Types and time-currents

The period that follows was Idealism. Ueberweg called it the "Age of Speculative Systems (until 1831)" (iv 1923, 4); Vollenhoven named Immanuel Kant, Johann Fichte, Friedrich Schelling, and Georg F. Hegel as its outstanding representatives.

---

18. Translator's note: Figure 4 lists Diderot as a materialist in the age of the Enlightenment but not Voltaire or Rousseau, who are neither Spinozists nor Thomists.

Late Rationalism commenced with positivism (that of Auguste Comte and others); Van den Berg (aligning himself with Étienne Gilson) characterized this movement as the time of "intellectual asceticism" and as literary realism—after Romanticism (1984, 207–18). In addition to Comte, Vollenhoven selected John Stuart Mill, Charles Darwin, and Ludwig Feuerbach as its representatives.

Around 1900, following neo-Enlightenment and neo-Idealism, the Irrationalism of the twentieth century emerged.

These time-currents, as designated by Vollenhoven, can be seen in Van den Berg's book, partly in the citations mentioned above, partly in other references.

B. THREE TYPES

Three types are represented in Figure 4, namely, Spinozism, materialism, and Thomism. The materialistic type starts with Democritus, who lived in ancient Greece, and continues to Monod in the twentieth century. Thomists, whom I designated somewhat boldly with a halo above their heads, are found in the entire historical period from Thomas Aquinas to the neo-Thomists. And in the Spinozistic tradition, Vollenhoven located about fifteen representatives in the five time-currents listed (cf. 1962d), with Albert Einstein, who more than once appealed to Spinoza, appearing last in our illustration.

C. CONCEPTIONS

My diagrams may suggest that these differences are a matter of composure and emotional temperament, but the nub of the question actually has to do with the principle of each respective conception. On the one hand, each conception is unique, and, on the other hand, each has two kinds of relations, namely, types and time-currents, or vertical and horizontal temporal connections. The term *network-historiography* has also been used.

We shall use the conception of Denis Diderot (1713–1784) as an example of these two kinds of relations. None will doubt that Diderot, one of the main editors of the renowned and monumental *Encyclopédie*, was a protagonist of the Enlightenment. But his manner of thinking, namely, his special type or ontology, is much less known.[19] He may be labeled a

---

19. Diderot 1956; Ueberweg iii, 430–32; Torrey 1967, 397–403; Winter 1972; De Fontenay 1981.

materialist, as long as the term is used in a broad sense. According to Diderot, all matter consisting of atoms possesses sensitivity. This is not a property originating within a certain complexity, but it is inherent to matter itself—it's part of the atom.

Diderot's view can also be said to be a kind of naturalism[20] in the sense of an organic worldview, an "all-living universe" (G. *die Allbelebtheit des Universums*). Biologism is another option, as there is a kinship with Julien de La Mettrie's *L'Homme Plante*, "the human plant."[21] Vollenhoven spoke of a phytological interactionism (Gk. *phyton* "plant"). Diderot wrote the following in a love letter:

> Oh, Sophia, my darling! . . . [Should] in the course of the centuries I again become one with you, if the molecules of your lover turned to dust could be stirred again and could search for yours which have been scattered in nature! Permit me this phanthom, which fills me with a sweet feeling, and promises me eternity, in and with you. (1950, 15 October 1759)

If these molecules could unite themselves in love—that's how an atheist who believed in ensouled matter described the life hereafter.

D. VIEWS CONCERNING HORIZONTAL AND VERTICAL LINES

"Holism" and "Pluralism"

As for the horizontal lines, Van den Berg and Foucault interpreted historical periods as massive unities. But several authors reject such a holistic view. The art historian Ernst Gombrich objected to a "holistic approach in terms of changing cultural styles,"[22] and the American historian Maurice Mandelbaum honored a "cultural pluralism," a diversity of traditions in a certain era, and "regards the fabric of historical occurrences as containing many strands."[23]

Vollenhoven, as we saw, distinguished both different successive (partially overlapping) time-currents with their own character and a pluralism of diverging traditions. One could designate his view, in this parlance, as a pluralistic holism.

---

20. Both Ueberweg and Torrey spoke of *naturalism* in this context.
21. Ueberweg, too, refers to the influence of La Mettrie and to Diderot's proximity to naturalism (iii, 431).
22. Gombrich 1978, 29. In this connection, the adjective *holistic* is derived from daily usage (cf. Bril 1986, 44f., 325). The term, as is known, also has other connotations.
    The German cultural historian Hans Schoeps also talks about "pluralism," that is, an "investigation of the *Zeitgeist*," which "cuts across many worldviews" (1959, 23, 58).
23. Mandelbaum 1965, 50–51. He usually designated *holism* as "sociological monism."

Philosophers as Song Birds?
Paradigm Switches and Transformations in Types

Concerning the vertical lines, some authors consider types, or thought traditions, to be constant. The Canadian philosopher F. F. Centore, for instance, distinguished six metaphysical paradigms, which he designated as "rather perennial possibilities." Another author spoke of "the same abstract idea that survives in history from generation to generation, always identifiable to the eye of the historian" (Spitzer 1944, 209–10). The classicalist Harry Wolfson likewise strongly emphasized possible agreements between philosophers from different eras (1947, 106). He compared these with song birds: "some of the [philosophers] philosophize as birds sing, without being aware that they are repeating ancient tunes." And yet types, as much as time-currents, can be conceived of holistically. Thomas Kuhn spoke of paradigm switches, designated as revolutions (e.g., the "Darwinian revolution"). Vollenhoven, too, viewed types (and type-complexes) as not being constant. In the mythological occult traditions, the Renaissance occultists maintained their own character, which differed from both the ancient (cf. Yates 1978) and the modern Gnostics. In the Thomistic tradition, from Thomas Aquinas to the neo-Thomists, Vollenhoven named representatives for different time-currents, e.g., from neo-Idealism, the Philosophy of Life, and Existentialism. Should a representative within a thought tradition arise in a following time-current, then one can speak of a new interpretation or of a transformation of the type.[24]

Thus, family resemblances contain family contrasts in horizontal as well as in vertical lines; in both, there is pluralism, not holism. Vollenhoven's method can be characterized, briefly, as a pluralistic diasynchrony.

Is a Time-Current a Dominant Type?

Sometimes a type or a complex of types dominates, as in the Gothic period, which was simultaneously a flourishing period of Aristotelianism. In the Renaissance, the occult tradition experienced a revival; afterward, this tradition existed for a considerable time as a subculture. One can ask whether in a given period a time-current is the same as a certain dominant tradition or whether there is a difference between them. If the answer is yes, then what is the characteristic of a time-

---

24. Vollenhoven usually spoke of *omwerken*, of a type being "rewritten" in a following time-current; elsewhere as "bent" and a few times as "transposed" ("Steffens" *OE*).

current and of a type? To answer this question, we must study Vollen-hoven's method "from the inside out."

The relation between external and internal aspects in time-currents is important (see Part One). In this regard, Vollenhoven also underscored the importance of the question regarding the founding of normativity, of good and evil, and of right and wrong. He spoke of the "place of the law," a topic to which we shall return in Part Four.

What precisely are types and how many are there? In the existing literature, there is no unanimity regarding their number. The English philosopher Charles Broad spoke of seventeen possible types,[25] Centore distinguished six. Once again, the question arises concerning the criterion for what constitutes a type and the method involved in such an investigation. But before tackling this question, we review, in Part Three, the main types Vollenhoven identified.

---

25. Translator's note: Broad wrote: "It appears to me that seventeen different types of metaphysical theory are possible theoretically on the relation between Mind and Matter" (1925, 606). Of these, he went on to say, only seven types have strong and weak points (ibid, 640–53).

PART THREE

TYPES

I. A Typological Survey

Introduction: A Sixth Attempt

Almost a century ago, (1925) Charles Broad spoke of "*seventeen* different types of metaphysical theory." About twenty years later, Vollenhoven set out once again to map the structures of Western thought, all the while placing his clarifications in continual confrontation with historical material. This was certainly not an idle aim. Before he developed his narrowly defined problem-historical method, he had made at least five other attempts to present a detailed arrangement of the entire field. His method was the result of years of prolonged research with its own ups and downs.[1] Even after establishing his first typological survey according to the problem-historical method, he continued to test and revise its results beyond his eightieth birthday. In pursuing his survey, however, he paid more attention to the actual investigation than to an explanation of his method. It is also true that he was more a researcher than a pedagogically gifted teacher. He set forth his method in a fuller sense only twice, namely in two Dutch articles, which were recently translated into English as "Conservatism and Progressiveness in Philosophy" (1959) and "The Problem-Historical Method" (1961).[2]

Dualism and Monism: The "Vertical Structure"

For Vollenhoven, questions about the make-up and constitution of things, about what some have called the unity and diversity of the "func-

---

1. Zuidema distinguished three periods in Vollenhoven's thinking (1963, 138); in the second period (as Zuidema put it), Vollenhoven himself distinguished four parts (1941k, 65, n. 2). If we combine these two givens, then we have six phases (cf. also Hart 1965, 4). We are interested in the final phase alone.
2. See Vollenhoven, *The Problem-Historical Method and the History of Philosophy*, forthcoming.

tions" of "functors" (Hart 1984)—is this philosopher a monist or a dualist?—are questions having to do with the *vertical structure* of things. For example, Vollenhoven designated the view in which the soul is the "the higher" part and the body the "lower" as a perspective about the "vertical structure" of things. Types have to do with the vertical structure of things and are *prima facie* either dualistic or monistic.

Anthropological dualism is still alive and well, but it does have well-established roots. It was documented as early as the fragments of Pythagoras, who espoused the doctrine of the migration of the soul, which, coming from elsewhere, unites itself with a body.[3] Begemann called Pythagoras "the father of dualism" (1975, 144). But dualism need not imply the doctrine of the transmigration of the soul. The basic idea of dualism is that things are binary; to which monism counters that, no, things are of one piece.

The soul, in the dualistic view, does not originate from the body but finds its origin elsewhere. Some of the church fathers were of the opinion that God created the soul separately and then united it with the body; Thomas Aquinas was of the same opinion (Sassen 1961, 131). This is called the doctrine of creatianism (not to be confused with creationism).

Tertullian (c. A.D. 200), one of the most remarkable figures from the early church, adopted an entirely different point of view regarding the soul's origin.[4] He rejected creatianism and instead accepted traducianism, which holds that both the soul and the body of a human being originate from the parents.[5] In other words, he advocated monism, a standpoint that has had many adherents in the Lutheran church.

According to Vollenhoven, there are several widely diverging monistic and dualistic types. But when studying the pertinent texts, one can easily make mistakes, as the following example from the Romantic period shows. At that time, a favorite term was *polarity*, which implied some kind of duality (which is not always the same as a dualism). A number of years ago, Brigitte Hoppe discussed the work of both J. von Görres, for whom "unity . . . originates from the interaction of dualities," and L. Oken, for whom there was "unity at the beginning of the universe, which splits into a 'duality'" (1967, 380). Von Görres accepted

---

3. A more recent explanation: a Dutch psychiatrist, Lietaert Peerbolte (1968, 26, 183, 188, 190, and 278; 1971, 28; 1974, 110), submitted that there is a "psi-layer" around the earth, from where the reincarnating souls descend.
4. Praamsma 1979, I, 55.
5. For creatianism and traducianism, see "Religion" in *RGG* I, 415 (cf. *HWP* iv, 1193, also for creatianism).

an original duality (dualism), while Oken embraced an original unity (monism). Oken's monism holds for his understanding of the universe as well. For Vollenhoven, the terms *monism* and *dualism,* likewise, refer to one's view of humanity and the cosmos.

According to Vollenhoven, every type, for example, the theory of interactionism, has its own view concerning the nature of "the vertical structure of things" (in free translation, an ontology). This implies also a view of the relation between "kingdoms," i.e., between matter and plants, plants and animals, and animals and humans.[6]

A Survey of the Five Main Typological Categories

I shall select four sequential citations from Vollenhoven's 1959 article "Conservatism and Progressiveness in Philosophy," in which he takes a closer and more concise look at his method. I shall interrupt his explanation with marginal notes containing examples. I will also add a fifth category (E). These five points are discussed under the headings A to E below. Schematically, the entire citation can easily be sketched, a handy feature we gladly demonstrate (see Figure 5).

A	MYTH (M)		COSMOGONIC (CG)						COSMOLOGICAL (CL)	
B	DUAL	MON	DUALISM		MONISM				DUALISM	MONISM
C				PRIOR.	INTERACT.		PARALL.			
D		AND	ANT		ANT	ZOO	PHY	LIM	UN	
E										

AND=ANDROLOGICAL   ZOO=ZOOLOGICAL   LIM=LIMITED
ANT=ANTHROLOGICAL   PHY=PHYTOLOGICAL   UN=UNLIMITED

Figure 5 Approaches to Structure

Here is the first part of Vollenhoven's citation:

> . . . a philosophical *conception* deals with two main problems: the position of the law and the vertical structure of the kingdoms. . . . I [now] wish to say something about the second question.
> This question implies several different things.

---

6. The terms *vertical higher and lower* can pertain to the relationship between kingdoms, the animal kingdom presupposing the plant kingdom, for instance. In some conceptions, such as those of the Gnostics or Anabaptists, these terms can imply a value judgment (the fall of the soul into matter).

41

[A] In the first place one must consider whether someone has approached the intended structure via myth, or whether one has considered structure (while rejecting myth as a source of philosophy) in a cosmogonic-cosmological or purely cosmological way.

[B] Furthermore there is the question of dualism and monism. (1959a, 43–44)

A. THE FIRST CATEGORY

The first of the five categories in the history of philosophy comprises three main groups: the mythologizing, the cosmogonic-cosmological, and the purely cosmological groups. Each main group, in turn, contains dualistic and monistic types (as we sketched above). Following a brief circumscription of the three main groups, we shall consider a characteristic theology in each of these.

Vollenhoven reckoned Platonism to be one view that belongs to the cosmogonic main group. We recall Alfred North Whitehead's famous adage: "The safest general characterization of the European philosophical tradition is that it consists of a series of footnotes to Plato" (1929, 63). Literally, the term *cosmogony* means the "becoming of the cosmos." This tradition especially emphasizes temporal changes and developments. Consistent evolutionism originates in this main group.

Vollenhoven deemed Aristotelianism especially and Thomism—which is indirectly connected to it—as expressing the purely cosmological main group.[7] Also, Scholasticism in a wider sense is reckoned to be part to this main group—in this tradition, according to Vollenhoven, one proceeds much more from a static cosmos than from a cosmogonic whole.

Earlier, I mentioned the mythologizing main group. One also speaks of the occult tradition (Poortman 1978) and of Gnosticism, which Gilles Quispel designated as "the third component of Europe's cultural tradition."[8]

1. Purely Cosmological Thinking: The Unmoved Mover

The Aristotelian tradition embraces a purely cosmological position. Aristotle's theology, for example, included the notion of the deity as the unmoved mover, that is, as the unchanging deity.[9] Traces of this notion[10]

---

7. Concerning purely cosmological thinking and creation, see note 14 on page 43.

8. This is the subtitle of Quispel's study (1988).

9. Translator's note: Aristotle, *Metaphysics* 1071b 4: an "eternal unmovable substance," and 1072a 24–25: "something which moves without being moved, being eternal."

are left in Roman Catholic and Protestant Scholasticism. Should one object to this interpretation by pointing out that God "repents," then the reply is: "This is merely an anthropomorphic way of speaking about God. Being, as a matter of fact, is unchangeable." Neither Vollenhoven nor his close associates like Klaas Popma and G. Visee had the slightest inclination to accept this theory. Visee wrote, as early as 1953, that believers ought to reverently use the language of the Holy Spirit.[11] And regarding the question about God repenting—specifically, the Scholastic denial of it—Popma remarked:

> Those questions [e.g., How can God's repentance agree with his unchange-ableness?] have a deadly ring to them and lead to dead ends. They are a convincing sign of not being willing to listen to the fructifying Word of God. For that Word says that God is "disappointed."[12]

Luther had a strong aversion to Aristotle. In a letter dated February 8, 1517, he wrote about him: "I am on nothing as keen as on unmasking, in the eyes of all, that clown who cheated the church with his Greek mask" (Boendermaker 1982, 50). Nevertheless, Scholasticism retained a following even in Protestant circles.[13]

The ancient Aristotelian notions regarding the eternity of the world clearly belong to a purely cosmological way of thinking.[14]

---

10. Translator's note: Augustine also embraced the doctrine of divine immutability. Cf. *The City of God*, Book 11, Chapter 21, where he wrote: "For He [God] does not pass from this to that by transition of thought, but beholds all things with absolute unchangeable-ness" or Book 8, Chapter 11: "Him that truly is, because He is unchangeable."

   Concerning this notion of immutability, see A. P. Bos (1991a, 120), who pointed out a kinship between Augustine and Parmenides on this score, evident in his famous procla-mation "Being *is*." According to Vollenhoven, Parmenides, the late Aristotle, Plotinus, and the late Augustine all belonged to the influential type of "purely cosmological think-ers" (2000, 201, 198, 240, and 236; cf. 1970a, 3).

11. By which he meant the language of Scripture. Visee 1979, 1, 45 ff.; cf. 1982, 2, 213–20.

12. Popma 1965, vii, 38. Translator's note: Popma wrote these words in the context of God's wrath against human sin threatening humanity (dust) with utter annihilation. Citing, in passing, Genesis 6:6: "And the Lord was sorry that he had made man on the earth, and it grieved him to his heart." In a similar context of God's anger with human sin, we read in 1 Samuel 15:11 and 35 that "the LORD repented that he had made Saul king over Israel."

13. On the other hand, the adjective *unchanging*, in the biblical sense, is used of God's reliabil-ity and faithfulness (1 Corinthians 1:9; 10:13), which remains even if a person loses his mind or is condemned to death as in the case of Stephen (Acts 7:56). The God of the Bible is not an "unmoved mover."

14. In connection with the eternity of the world and creation: The Dutch Socinian philoso-pher Frans Kuypers (c. 1660) maintained, for example, that eternal matter was there at God's disposal when he created the world. This motif of the world's eternity first ap-pears in Aristotle's works, later in the writings of Philoponos (first phase, c. 520), and

2. Cosmogonic Thinking: Process Theology

Process thinkers go back to Alfred North Whitehead and his successor Charles Hartshorne. In *Process and Reality* (1929), Whitehead looked at the world as a permanent transitional process toward new actualizations and concretizations.[15] In this process, God participates as the "great companion," as "the fellow-sufferer who understands" (ibid., 532). One cannot merely say that the world creates itself, but must also affirm that "It is as true to say that God creates the World, as that the World creates God" (ibid., 528). Process theology strives to conquer ". . . the (traditional theistic) picture of an unchanging, absolute Deity."[16] Other authors point to the contrast with the Scholastic tradition. Wildiers, for instance, wrote that Whitehead prefers to designate ultimate reality "with the term *fact, event,* whereas Aristotle and Thomas prefer the word *ousia, ens.*" Wildiers continued, "The God of process philosophy is first of all most intimately connected with the world. He is not a god outside of cosmic reality."[17]

Cosmogonic thinking constitutes a sharp contrast with purely cosmological thinking, which embraces more or less a static world, an

---

still later in the works of the Arabian philosophers Avicenna and Averroës, as well as those of the Jewish philosopher Levi ben Gerson (died 1344). Kuypers and the Renaissance philosopher Pomponazzi honored this point of view.

While at times a Christian philosopher partly agrees with this point as held, for instance, by Aristotle, such a synthesis philosophy (see p. 93) also contains integral or partly Biblical features, for instance, concerning the creation of the world.

In his earlier *Summa contra gentiles,* Thomas speaks about creation as temporal (2:31, 36 [6]), for there cannot be two eternities according to the Catholic faith (ibid, 2, 38 [8, 16]). In his later *Summa Theologiae* (I, 67–), he holds to a creation in "six days." In *ST* I, Article 46, Thomas states "That the world began is therefore an object of faith, not a proof or science." "God exists before the world in eternity, not in time." "When we say 'God created heaven and earth in the beginning' of time, we mean that earth and sky were created together with time, not that the action of creation was itself in time."

But in *De aeternitate mundi contra murmurantes,* Aquinas speaks of "the possibility of an eternal creation" (see the article, "Eternity of the World," in *HWP* ii, 843–47); creation (dependence) and eternity of the world are not contradictions (Lindberg, 1992, 233).

Cf. Wissink 1990, 136; and Bril in Vollenhoven 2000, 330–32 "Louter kosmologisch denken."

15. This example and most of the following examples that reference Vollenhoven's distinctions are not from Vollenhoven himself but concur with his typology. In Part One, I spoke about Vollenhoven's "maps and charts" on the one hand and on the other about the historic landscape. As for the map, Vollenhoven reckoned Whitehead's conceptualization to a (monistic) cosmogonic way of thinking (1962d, 46).

16. Dalferth, in *HWP* vii, 1562–65.

17. Wildiers 1985, 64, 86. For process theology, Cobb 1965; Griffin 1990; Meuleman 1974; and Meinema 1989.

eternal(ized) reality. In the ancient world of the Greeks, Parmenides was one of the ancestors of a purely cosmological perspective. According to him, "being" is immutable and immobile, with neither beginning nor end. The changes we perceive are mere semblance. In contrast, Heraclitus was one of the early advocates of a cosmogonic viewpoint, which maintains the slogan "all things are in flux" (Gk. *panta rhei*). Nothing "is," everything becomes or is in motion. "One cannot step into the same river twice." Both contrasting viewpoints appear to be very ancient and persistent. As Milic Capek summarized when writing about "change" (1967): "Although the dialogue between Parmenides and Heraclitus [between the metaphysics of being and of becoming] is still going on, the former is now less favored than the latter."[18]

The tension between these two pre-Socratics is also found 150 years later, at the culmination of Greek philosophy, namely, between Plato and Aristotle.

Whereas Plato explained that the world came into being through the work of the divine craftsman or demiurge, Aristotle, in contrast, argued that the cosmos had to be unchanging or without a beginning. To speak of the creation of the world is to violate God's self-sufficiency and immutability. Aristotle, therefore, rejected the notion of a world creator, reasoning that the cosmos is from all eternity, without beginning and change.[19]

3. Mythological, Theogonic Thinking

The third main group, the mythologizing tradition, espouses a theogonic way of thinking (the beginning and the generations of the deities). It is very much present in Gnosticism (c. 150 A.D.). There is a most high but completely unknown god. Below him are several aeons—spiritual, divine beings—which, directly or indirectly, originated from the most high god by way of emanation (an outpouring). Eventually, one of the aeons, lady Sophia, caused a breach in the worlds of gods and

---

18. As we said, Vollenhoven also used the term *static thinking* instead of *purely cosmological thinking* ("Witnessing in Science," in Tol and Bril), often even concerning matter. He himself interpreted physical nature, the plant and animal kingdoms, as a coming into being. He judged the notion of the constancy of species to be of Aristotelian origin ("Problems Concerning Time," in Tol and Bril).

    After the discovery of radioactivity (1896) and the fallout in the core of the atom—evidence that matter was not constant—soon after the turn of the century, scientists spoke of the "metaphysical bomb called radium" (Bowler 1988, 194).

19. So A. P. Bos 1991a, 79–81, and 1991b, 55–58.

humans, a breach with the most high god. In addition, Gnosticism recognizes a negatively qualified creator of the earth, the demiurge, who in Jewish and Christian Gnosticism often is identified with Yahweh, the God of the Old Testament. Besides, there are rulers (Gk. *archontes*), lower cosmic, spiritual, and evil powers. Humans, who have fallen from the higher, divine world and landed into the realm of evil matter, can be saved from this evil world through higher knowledge (Gk. *gnosis*).

In contrast, Zandee pointed to the first article of the Apostles' Creed—"I believe in God the Father almighty," the God who is also the "Maker of heaven and earth" (1965, 23). Here "we recognize a dispute with the Gnostic doctrine concerning the demiurge." This resistance to Gnosticism is, likewise, expressed at the conclusion of the Creed, "I believe . . . the resurrection of the body."[20]

Among the Gnostics, there was a great diversity of theogonies. Manicheism, of which Augustine in his younger years was a temporary follower and which spread from Mesopotamia to the Atlantic Ocean in the West and to China in the East, appeared to have a complex theogony as well.

The Jews have their own mythological tradition, the Kabbala. The most important kabbalistic writing is the *Zohar*, whose origin has now at last, in the twentieth century, been traced to northern Spain (c. 1280).

---

20 Apostolicum and Gnosticism. The "rule of faith," from which the Apostles' Creed later originated, is found as early as the church father Irenaeus (A.D. 170) (cf. Praamsma 1979, I, 53 for a Dutch translation). For the origin of the Apostles' Creed and its relation to Gnosticism, see also Kelly (1972); Steubing 1977, 13; and the controversial book by Elaine Pagels 1981 (under "Apostolic Creeds").

In his study concerning the origin of Christian doctrine, Maurice Wiles pointed out that Gnosticism was the greatest challenge for the church of the second century (1975, 101). Earlier, he wrote: "the influence of heresy on the early development of doctrine is so great that it is almost impossible to exaggerate it" (ibid, 36).

The Apostles' Creed is part of the confession of both the Roman Catholic Church and of the churches of the Reformation. Qua origin, the "rule of faith" is the oldest of the confessions. We think of the Latin phrase *In necessariis unitas, in non necessariis libertas, in utrisque caritas* ("In the necessary things unity, in the nonnecessary things freedom, and love in both").

The English theologian Alister E. McGrath (1996, 23) attributed this striking phrase to Richard Baxter (d. 1691), who, along with the German pietist Jacob Spener (d. 1705) referred to this slogan on more than one occasion. In 1931, however, Albert Eekhof, professor in Leiden (d. 1933), demonstrated in detail that this slogan antedated by twenty-five years the reference in Baxter's work, for Rupertus Meldinus, a pseudonym for Petrus Meiderlinus (1582–1651), coined it in *Paraenesis votiva* (1626).

This view appears clearly linked to the view of John Calvin (*Institutes of the Christian Religion* IV.1.12; so Breman 1998, 442, n. 42). Eekhof, too, points to a kinship with Calvin (1931, 55–56). Cf. *RGG* 4 (1960) 845; Schilder 1960, 127–142; Berkouwer 1972, 98.

This mysterious writing mentions a wholly unknown God (Hebrew *En Sof*),[21] who resides above the ten divine aeons (Hebrew *sefirot*), which originated, by way of emanation, from *En Sof*. These independent, divine properties created the world. Azriel of Gerona (early thirteenth century) has the following illustration. The Bible knows of only ten *sefirot*, God the Creator, and above him *En Sof*. Through an allegorical exegesis of the Old Testament, one can support any form of Gnosticism, for all Muslim, Christian, and Jewish forms of Gnosticism embrace an allegorical exegesis.

About 250 years after the founding of the Kabbala, a new center of gravity appeared in Saphed in Upper Galilee. After many years, Gnostic thinking, surprisingly, had not weakened but rather had become stronger. Jewish Gnosticism gained influence in the hermetical Kabbalism of the Renaissance; afterward, Hasidism was also found in the kabbalistic tradition (Scholem 1954, 325ff.). Mention can also be made of hermetical kabbalism[22] at the time of the Renaissance as well as of the occult tradition during the next three centuries.

I was surprised to discover that Max Heindel (1865–1919), the founder of *The Rosicrucian Fellowship*, had composed a very complicated theogony. He held that beyond Jehovah and the God of our solar system exists the Absolute, the One. From the One originated seven large *Logoi* in the first cosmic realm; from each of these, in turn, another seven *Logoi* originated in the second cosmic realm; in the third cosmic realm seven times seven times seven deities originated; until the seventh cosmic realm—a very great fiction. Each of the solar systems, including our solar system (the demiurge), had its own deity. In the realm below resided the spirits of the seven planets, the Father, the Son, Jehovah, the Holy Spirit, and the guide of the moon (Heindel 1925, 178, 377, 403). The theosophist Blavatsky and polytheist Rudolf Steiner, the spiritual ancestor of the Free Schools, mentioned heavenly hierarchies originating from one another as well.

Among the ancient Greeks, we mentioned one ancestor of purely cosmological thinking (Parmenides) and one of cosmogonic thinking (Heraclitus). Hesiod, it appears, is the oldest representative of theogonic, mythologizing thinking (cf. the title of one of his main works, *Theogony*).[23]

---

21. The kabbalist expert Gershom Scholem explains: "In order to express this unknowable aspect of the Divine the early kabbalists of Provence and Spain coined the term *Ein-Sof* ('Infinite')" (1974, 88).
22. Yates 1978, 86, 106.
23. Cf. Popma 1963, 16–43; A. P. Bos 1991a.

Simply reviewing each of the three main groups is a bit bewildering. Probing into the history of the West is seldom a form of entertainment. Yet such probing may be necessary if we are to gain insight into the background of the world in which we live today. With his analyses, Vollenhoven attempted to be helpful in this orientation.

B. THE SECOND CATEGORY: DUALISM AND MONISM

In his first quotation (concerning cosmological, cosmogonic, and mythologizing thinking), Vollenhoven next discussed the terms *dualism* and *monism*:

> [B] Furthermore there is the question of dualism and monism. In other words, one can think that everything is based on the eternal correlation of the transcendent and the nontranscendent, such that any unity must be explained in connection to these two categories with the result that unity is derivative. Alternatively, one can postulate that everything is at bottom a unity and consequently that any difference must be ascribed to divergence. (1959a, 44)

We introduced the second category (on p. 39) when discussing anthropology. If we combine these givens with the three main groups just discussed, then we can make the following observation. In the main type of dualistic mythologizing thinking, the notion of *reincarnation* is often found; in the main type of dualistic purely cosmological thinking, *creatianism* is frequently encountered; and especially in the monistic cosmogonic way of thinking, *traducianism* occurs.[24]

A Few Dualistic and Monistic Theologies

(1) The Aristotelian tradition is cosmological and dualistic. The unmoved mover, or "thought thinking itself" (Gk. *noesis tes noeseos*) transcends (Lat. *transcendere* "overstep"), or surpasses, the world.

(2) Within the cosmogonic line of thinking, the theology of Spinoza was avowedly monistic. For he affirmed "God or nature" (Lat. *deus sive natura*), God being equal to nature.

(3) In mythologizing thinking, too, there are dualistic and monistic systems. The difference here truly stands out. Again, dualism starts from an original duality, monism proceeds from a primordial unity.

Manicheism, a famous religion, is strictly dualistic. According to its adherents, originally there were two principles: light, the good principle,

---

24. This is a global approach. Reincarnation and creatianism, for instance, occur also in cosmogonic dualism.

or the "Father of Greatness" living in the realm of light, and darkness, "the Ruler of Darkness."

There is also a longstanding theological tradition in monistic my-thologizing thinking that includes the Gnostic Valentinus (c. A.D. 100–160) and Jakob Böhme (1575–1624). Here the principles of good and evil, of light and darkness (shadow) are aspects of one and the same primeval unity. The same is true for psychiatrist Carl Jung (1875–1961), who rejected God as triune and maintained that evil is present within God.[25] As R. J. van Helsdingen, an expert on Jung, wrote, "God is not so much a triad as a tetrade: the divine couple, namely, the Father and the Mother, along with their two sons or antagonistic brothers—the devil and Christ—and as the fifth essence, the Holy Spirit coming from this tetrade."[26]

C. "THE PROBLEM OF THE VERTICAL RELATIONSHIP . . ."

To understand the following example, we need the third and the fourth or final categories, as the continuation of Vollenhoven's first quotation shows:

> [C] In the third place there is the problem of the vertical relationship, in dual-ism between the transcendent and the non-transcendent, and in monism between the higher and lower species of the original unity.
> [D] Finally we must determine the site within which a dualist posits the boundary between the transcendent and the nontranscendent, and in which the monist posits the single origin of everything. (1959a, 44)

In accordance with Vollenhoven's quotation, we shall discuss, within cosmogonic thinking, first the difference between andrological and an-thropological dualism.

Dualism and "The Nature of the Woman"

Within mythologizing and cosmogonic dualism, Vollenhoven distin-guished two types: andrological and anthropological dualism (cf. 1962d). The adjective *andrological* (Gk. *andros logos* "the study of man") signifies that men, in contrast to women, share in transcendence. In these "charts," Vollenhoven listed the names of the time-currents and types as

---

25. The specific example is my own, but Vollenhoven did place Jung in the line of monistic mythologizing thinkers (see "Orfiek" and "Parallellisme" *OE* and 1962d, 41).

26. Van Helsdingen 1983, 147. It is worth noting that Jung wrote a preface to one of Van Helsdingen's early books (*CW* 18/59, 1252–55). See further Jung's Gnostic "Seven Ser-mons to the Dead" (the dead being the Christians) and his "Answer to Job."

well as the names of different representatives. As for andrological thought, in the modern period he mentioned only Otto Weininger, about whom, as far as I know, he devoted only a few lines in his lecture (1958d, 11), labeling him a supporter of andrological dualism coupled with the notion of reincarnation. But in this instance and in other instances, it is desirable to consult the author personally.

Otto Weininger (1880–1903) received his doctorate at age twenty-two with a bulky dissertation titled "Sex and Character" (*Geschlecht und Charakter*). The following year, it appeared in book form and shortly thereafter in French, Italian, and English translations (we have consulted the 1932 German edition). Well-known figures like Georg Simmel, Henri Bergson, Arnold Schönberg, and August Strindberg studied his work with interest.

In Chapter Twelve of his dissertation, titled "The Essence of Womanhood . . .," the author wrote that in the case of women, "thinking and feeling are one, they are not separate; with men, they are distinct" (1932, 122). Among women there is no genuine genius (419). The difference between men and women is found in the difference between earthly and higher forms of life (441). He talks about ". . . the complete nothingness of feminine life, its thorough lack of a higher being" (377). Lacking a soul, women participate in eternal life no more than other organisms (382–83; cf. 252, 390). Only men are free from the natural laws (436) and can turn to that which is timeless (426), possessing as they do a higher monad. Summarizing his point of view, Weininger wrote:

> And yet, the absolute woman, who lacks individuality and a will, and who has no part in values and love, is, we can put it thus, excluded from every higher, transcendent, and metaphysical being. The intelligible, supra-empirical existence of men is elevated above matter, space and time; for men being mortal as well as being immortal is sufficient. (374)

Weininger made two vertical distinctions: between higher and lower and between transcendence and nontranscendence. In anthropological dualism, both men and women possess a monad, a higher, transcendent soul, "a soul with a fine material body"; in andrological thinking, the accent (the level) is different: only men or some men have a transcendent soul. When one studies the relevant texts, the circumscription of Vollenhoven's third point about the vertical relationship within dualism, or transcendence and non-transcendence, becomes clear. This concerns also his fourth point—the level of the distinction between men and women or the boundary between transcendence and nontranscendence.

Weininger had a remarkable view (to which we shall return in the next section) concerning the solution of the problem of woman: ". . . thus, women must cease to be women and become men" (452); "Negation, overcoming womanhood, that is the issue" (453); ". . . the woman as such must perish" (455). But "the woman can hardly achieve such a goal in her own strength" (455).[27]

W. F. Hermans, a Dutch author, noted that "many significant men earnestly sought to get to know Weininger's ideas" (1984). After Weininger's death (1903), August Strindberg wrote about *Sex and Character*: "a mightily inspiring book, which probably solved the most difficult of all problems." The famous philosopher Ludwig Wittgenstein, apparently, was an admirer of Otto Weininger as well.[28]

A good eighty years after the publication of Weininger's book, the first Dutch translation appeared of *Sex and Character*. Mary Fahrenfort emphasized that it was a dangerous book, but W. F. Hermans was captivated by it.[29]

But was Weininger the first and sole author of such a view concerning women?

Weininger and *The Gospel of Thomas*

In his *Schematische Kaarten* (1962d, 2000), Vollenhoven mentioned several names in his rubric of andrological dualism. During antiquity, he listed the so-called *The Gospel of Thomas,* an apocryphal work that originated in postbiblical times, to which the name of Thomas was attached. Gilles Quispel spoke of Encratism, a movement with strongly ascetic tendencies. Some Encratists abstained from wine, others maintained a strictly vegetarian diet, and still others preached sexual abstinence. In contrast to Psalm 24:1, "The earth is the LORD's and the fullness thereof," the Encratists, according to Quispel, saw the created world and earthly life as evil, as a place of bondage from which believers may be delivered through an ascetic lifestyle (cf. Mantz-van der Meer 1989).

"The Gospel of Thomas" was discovered in its entirety in the famous library at Nag Hammadi in 1946 and was first disseminated in the West in

---

27. Even nations, like the English nation, can be inferior. While himself of Jewish descent, Weininger had strongly anti-Semitic ideas. "Nevertheless, humanity's predisposition in the Jews, more yet in the negroes, and still more in women, is saddled with a greater number of amoral drives" (449).
28. Monk's biography of Wittgenstein includes a good deal of information about Weininger's influence (1991, 19). See further Rider and Leser 1984.
29. *Trouw* August 2, 1984; *NRC-Handelsblad* July 27, 1984.

1956. All kinds of theories have been proposed concerning its date. The expert Tjitze Baarda has adopted the following working hypothesis: "Thomas is an anthology, a bouquet of proverbs of Jesus that someone selected from a variety of traditions, I suspect, between A.D. 140 and 200" (1999, 34; cf. 45, 28; also 2003).

Of the 114 *logia,* or proverbs, we shall cite four. (1) "Jesus said, 'Whoever has come to understand the world has found (only) a corpse, and whoever has found a corpse is superior to the world'" (#56). Schippers noted that in this logion "there is definitely an hostile attitude to the world" (1960, 109). (2) "Jesus said, 'If they say to you, "Where did you come from?" say to them, 'We came from the light, the place where the light came into being'" (#50). This saying stresses the soul's dualistic nature and transcendent origin. (3) And "Jesus said, 'Woe to the flesh that depends on the soul; woe to the soul that depends on the flesh'" (#112). Sayings 56 and 112 imply a rejection of what the Apostles' Creed confesses: "I believe in the resurrection of the flesh" (cf. Schippers, 130). (4) Saying 114 makes another point. "Simon Peter said to them, 'Let Mary leave us, for women are not worthy of Life.' Jesus said, 'I myself shall lead her in order to make her male, so that she may become a living spirit resembling you males. For every woman who will make herself male will enter the Kingdom of heaven.'" Centuries later, one hears, as it were, its echo in Weininger's conclusion: ". . . thus women must cease to be women and become men" (1902).

According to Quispel, *The Gospel of Thomas* was known to Mani (216–277 A.D.), the ancestor of Manicheism (1991, 31ff.). Messalians, members of a movement originating in Edessa, Syria (fourth century), who moved to Armenia and who in the Middle Ages were transferred to Bulgaria, knew the text as well. They influenced the Bulgarian Bogomiles who, in turn, affected the Cathari.[30] The Cathari believed in reincarnation and held to the doctrine of two principles as well. The God of the Old Testament, namely Satan, created the world.[31] Christ appeared in an apparent body (docetism) to teach humans the way to deliver themselves from matter through an ascetic and vegetarian lifestyle. Their beliefs about reincarnation prohibited perfect members from propagating the human race and demanded suicide by means of continual fasting. (Weininger, though us-

---

30. Van Schaik disagreed with Quispel and many others, arguing that no influence can be demonstrated between the Manicheans and the Cathari (2004, 92–93). There is an agreement, however, as far as ontology is concerned.
31. In his comments on "The Faith in Jehovah and the Doctrine of Moses," the anti-Semitic Weininger, wrote: "Jehovah is the personified idea of Judaism" (1932, 411).

ing somewhat different terminology, suggested similar instructions, as well as the ascetic practice.[32]) The Cathari, finally, coined the following remarkable proverb: "when . . . believing women die, they change into men";[33] this pronouncement recalls the above-mentioned logion 114 from *The Gospel of Thomas.* All in all, exploring the notion of andrological dualism, one finds, by repetition, *a complex of interrelated themes.*[34]

One finds these kinds of *clusters* in other types of thought, but then involving other themes, since each type has its own particular "problem-patterns" (Hart 1966, xii; see p. 61 below).[35]

The Problem of the Vertical Relation in Monism

We continue our marginal notes concerning the third problem in Vollenhoven's citation, namely, the "problem of the vertical relation," as it pertains to monism (following dualism).

In a philosophical anthropology, a duality or polarity between body and soul can have as its base either an original duality or an original unity. When human beings develop from a living cell, a distinction is often made between their psychic and somatic aspects. Some monists see *interaction* between these two, others propagate a *parallelism* between these two processes, while still others state that the higher aspect or the soul can influence the body—through a "downward causation" (cf. the neurologist R. W. Sperry). Vollenhoven called the latter the *theory of priority.*

---

32. For Weininger (1932) on: sexuality cf. 456; reincarnation 435; death as deliverance 374, also 435, 458; and his own ascetic tendencies 456, 459, and 379n.

33. Quispel 1991, 32.

34. Andrological dualism is found both in mythologizing and cosmogonic ways of thinking (Vollenhoven 1956b, 1962f), but we shall let go of this distinction here. Several types have mythologizing and cosmogonic variations.

35. Is there one type or are there two types? When Vollenhoven was almost seventy-eight years old, he wanted to speak of only one main type in this relevant dualism, instigated as he was by his old student Theo van der Merwe (Private lecture series 1971a, 46f.). We are of the opinion, however, that we have here two clearly separate types, each of these with its own ontology and a specific constellation of themes, which one can perceive again and again through Western history. Possibly another name is desirable for the type under discussion.

Clearly, andrological thinking can be retrieved in several types (cf. Concilium 21, 1985). In the pertinent type, for Weininger it concerns special people, for instance, the perfect ones among the Cathari and "the absolute man," in contrast to the empirical one.

For many years, Vollenhoven designated this type "phrenological," as in 1956b, 7, where he wrote about this dualistic type (in contrast to the other): "The one that accepts the theme of transmigration deems only the conscious reflection—Gk. *phren*—to be transcendent. That is why one can call this type 'pure phrenological.'" It appears that this view is usually developed andrologically, from *The Gospel of Thomas* to Weininger in 1902.

53

Thus, there are three views concerning the nature of the relation between the higher and the lower species arising out of a monistic origin (cf. 1964a). Or, as Vollenhoven sometimes formulated it, there are three viewpoints regarding the relation between the higher and lower as they diverge from the origin (e.g., separation in the process of becoming, as in embryology) (1964a, 218). To these differences we now turn.

D. THE FOURTH PROBLEM:
"HOW D'ALEMBERT DIFFERS FROM A COW" (DIDEROT)

More needs to be said about differences within dualism and monism. As noted earlier, Vollenhoven's citation ends as follows:

> [D] Finally we must determine the site within which a dualist posits the boundary between the transcendent and the nontranscendent, and in which the monist posits the single origin of everything.

As our discussion of Cathari and Weininger has made clear, there are difference among dualists. Types will differ on the distinct levels at which the main difference is located. As we have seen, anthropological dualism affirms that both men and women possess a transcendent soul, possibly a transcendent monad (a soul with a body of fine matter), allowing for reincarnation (Poortman 1978). Whereas andrological dualism maintains a higher boundary between transcendence and nontranscendence, only certain selected persons possess this higher consciousness.

So, too, there are different types of monism. For example, there prove to be three types of cosmogonic interactionary monists. Some monists assert that though there are differences between plants, animals, and humans, there are no essential differences. Humans are, in a certain sense, plants ("man, a plant," as La Mettrie wrote). Vollenhoven called this theory *phytological interactionism* (Gk. *phyton* "plant"). Denis Diderot, as we already saw (p. 35 above), held such a naturalistic standpoint, in the sense of a biologism. Concerning his friend d'Alembert, he wrote: "How d'Alembert differs from a cow . . . I cannot quite understand. But some day science will explain."[36] (The materialist continues to live in hope. In this connection Karl Popper saw, ironically, a "promissory materialism."[37]) Diderot did not want to remain in the dark, however, for he held that in the end even the atoms will be ensouled. With humans, it is merely a matter of higher complexities.

---

36. Torrey 1967, 400.
37. Popper and Eccles 1977, 96–98, 205.

According to the theory of zoological interactionism, there is basically no essential difference between humans and animals. Both possess feelings or consciousness, whereas plants do not. And feelings, strivings, can be a principal factor in evolution, in so-called psycho-Lamarckism.[38] The level at which the higher and lower is differentiated is, in this case, higher than in the preceding type.

Those who support the theory of anthropological interactionism see a fundamental difference between humans and animals. To them, the level of the distinction is again higher than in zoological interactionism.

In other words, the relationship between matter and the kingdoms of plants, animals, and humans concerns the distinction between higher and lower that is always one step up with plants, animals, and humans, respectively. To put it in a single phrase, it concerns the "relationship between kingdoms."

E. THE FIFTH CATEGORY: INDIVIDUALISM VERSUS MYSTICISM

Under the above-mentioned types (headings A-D), I discussed four of Vollenhoven's categories in connection with several points of view concerning the vertical structure of the kingdoms. From the beginning, however, Vollenhoven maintained a fifth category. This fifth category is related to another distinct problem category, namely that of the universal and the individual. Within each type of monism and dualism, Vollenhoven asked: is the nature of reality—monistically or dualistically conceived, as the case may be—borne only by individuals, or is it borne by a universal whole, or is it shared by individuals and the universal whole alike? Vollenhoven called these three options *individualism, universalism,* and *partial-universalism,* respectively. In connection with the last two, mysticism can occur. We shall look at this more closely.

Mysticism in one form or other does occur in each main type of monistic or dualistic thought distinguished by Vollenhoven. For instance, there is the mysticism espoused by Plotinus (A.D. 205–270),[39] which influenced the view of Meister Johannes Eckhart (1260–1327);[40] the Arabian philosopher Averroës (Ibn Ruschd, 1126–1198), who influenced Eckhart the Younger (or Eckhart of Gründig) in the late Middle

---

38. To distinguish from Lamarckism, or the heredity of acquired properties, a generally common view in the mid-1800s and also with Darwin.
39. Oosthuizen mentions sixteen studies concerning Plotinus' mysticism (1974, 70). Kenney (1991) considers mainly the "mystical monotheism of Plotinus."
40. Merlan 1960, 127.

Ages;[41] and the intellectual mysticism of Benedict Spinoza and the time-mysticism of Henri Bergson.[42] In other words, there is a great diversity of forms of mysticism.

What is mysticism? C. W. Mönnich described it as "the leveling of the distinction between God and humanity,"[43] a description that is not applicable to Buddhistic mysticism, which does not refer to God. Evelyn Underhill (1875–1941) insightfully circumscribed mysticism as "the science of union with the Absolute, and nothing else."[44] Others pointed to an oceanic feeling, an absorption of the individual into the universal. Vollenhoven defined it as follows:

> Philosophically, mysticism is a variation of universalism; as such, mysticism teaches that the universal precedes the individual, which originates from, or is a form of appearance of, the universal. To this universalistic main thought, mysticism adds that at the moment of death individual existence returns to the universal. ("Mystiek" OE)

The Jewish philosopher Martin Buber (1878–1965) opposed mysticism. He proceeded from the I–Thou relationship between God and humanity (Buber 1970) and rejected the kind of unified Being "beyond I and Thou" that mysticism—and universalism—would require. He once wrote, "In the reality which we experience, here is no unity of Being."[45] There are many who reject a consistent universalism. For example, Rosenzweig (1886–1929), another Jewish thinker, disposed of every formula, "Everything is . . ." (water: Thales; or fire: Heraclitus); God, humanity, and the world, for Rosenzweig, are three irreducible roots of every experience—three "original facts" (Goldenson 1962, 125–28).

In *partial universalism,* particulars (individuals) have their own identity alongside of universals. The latter may be a world soul, as, for instance, with the Arabian philosopher Averroës (1126–1198) and the German biologist Hans Driesch (some of whose works Vollenhoven carefully studied in the 1920s). There was also about the same time, for example, a Dutch psychologist, Gerard Heymans, who, working within this

---

41. Merlan 1976, 461–70 (cf. Bril 1986, 157–60, 320, concerning Vollenhoven's interpretation).
42. Popma 1963, 199–207.
43. "Mysticism," in the *Grote Winkler Prins* 16, 1982, 97.
44. Underhill 1955, 72 (according to Wetlesen 1978, 211).
45. Translator's note: 1923; *Werke* I, 1962, 134, 138. In his *Eclipse of God*, the author writes that religion "is not a relation to a Being or Reality, which . . . always remains transcendent." Religion is about the "relation of an I to a Thou" (New York, 1952, 79).

framework, explained parapsychological phenomena as "carrying over psychical contents within the world soul."[46]

Partial universalism maintains the *original correlation* between the individual and the universal, not merely a temporary independence of the individual away from the universal (the world soul). In other words, it does not view the individual (e.g., a human being) as a temporary offshoot of the universal (as is the case with universalism), and neither does it deny the existence of the universal (as does individualism).[47]

Consistent *individualism* accepts only individuals and rejects every thought of anything essentially universal. This led the Dutch theologian Haitjema to note that Max Stirner's individualism—for example, in his book *Der Einzige und sein Eigentum*—lacks a reasonable world order as well as ideal norms (1929, 24).

These few illustrations must suffice as an impression of Vollenhoven's last subdivision of types into three possible subtypes: individualism, partial universalism, and universalism, which in history acquired divergent results.

F. VOLLENHOVEN'S OWN STANDPOINT

As Vollenhoven's own point of view has been given attention elsewhere,[48] I shall limit myself to four marginal notes.

1. There is *a boundary between God and the cosmos*,[49] the ignoring of which makes all philosophizing about God speculative. Klaas Popma, Vollenhoven's close associate, repeatedly made the same point. Theo de Boer, one of Vollenhoven's students, who later went more his own way, did the same in a work whose title reiterates the well-known phrase of Blaise Pascal, "God of Abraham, God of Isaac, God of Jacob, not of the philosophers and the scholars": *De God van de filosofen en de God van Pascal* (1989).[50] Vollenhoven, Popma, and De Boer, in this respect, agree with

---

46. See Van Dongen and Gerding 1983, 37. Individual identity was actually of little importance for Heymans.
47. In a purely cosmological way of thinking (see p. 42 above), partial universalism assumes two very different forms: in ouranian mysticism, the universal is located in the higher (cf. Averroës); in telluric mysticism (e.g., of mother earth), the universal is found in the lower (cf. Klages). See Vollenhoven "Mystiek," in *OE* x, 415.
48. See Tol and Bril 1992, Chapters 1–10.
49. Vollenhoven 1941f §13; 1967b §13. Calvin pointed at the epistemological correlation between knowing God and knowing self and thus implied the distinction between Creator and creature (*Institutes* I.1–3).
50. Translator's note: This confession is part of a larger vision Pascal recorded on a parchment around November 23, 1654 (O'Connell 1997, 96).

Martin Buber's "There is no unity of being" and disagree with, for instance, Spinoza's dictum "God or nature."

Given our inability to transcend the boundary that marks off the cosmos from God, philosophical considerations are limited to the cosmos alone. In the created world, the individual and the universal do not exist in isolation, but that which is individual (human being, animal, or plant) and that which universal (modalities) can be distinguished. As Vollenhoven put it, ". . . the universal and the individual are features that everywhere intersect" (1956b, 11) (cf. the fifth criterion).

2. Concerning dualistic and monistic theologies, the Manicheans, whom we mentioned earlier, knew two original principles (not one). Such a dualism is also found among most of the myths of creation: "a creational struggle . . . [between] usually two original principles" (Von Rad 1955, 30). In contrast, there is the view that the world—and sometimes deities—came into being through emanation from God. "But therewith," Von Rad continued, "*the boundary between God and the world is effaced.*"

The biblical message concerning creation is neither dualistic nor monistic, as Vollenhoven summarized: ". . . the world is not a correlate to God, neither is it an emanation from His being. But it has been created by Him and is placed under His law" (1955ms, 5). And in another place, he wrote, "Christianity is neither dualistic nor monistic" (1964a, 218).

3. We call to mind the opposition of the Apostles' Creed to Gnosticism and recall the objections against the Aristotelian-Scholastic notion of the "unmoved mover."

4. In the preceding paragraphs, I supplied several answers to five important questions (explained under headings A-E above), namely, (A) the genesis of becoming, (B) dualism versus monism, (C) the relationship between the higher and the lower, (D) the demarcation, or boundary, between the higher and the lower, and (E) the connection between universality and individuality. To a great extent, Vollenhoven's own response to these answers is found in his theory regarding the kingdoms (of matter, plants, animals, and humans); the functions or the modalities; and the human heart, in the sense of the prefunctional moment of human life.[51]

---

51. Cf. Tol and Bril 1992, Part One; and *A Vollenhoven Reader*, forthcoming.

G. A GLANCE BACK

All Five Distinctions Together

Vollenhoven would designate Spinozism, as a tradition of thought in a typological sense, by means of the above-mentioned five categories as follows: (1) cosmogonic main group, (2) monism, (3) parallelism, (4) partial parallelism,[52] and (5) universalism (Bril 1986, 133–42). (Types often display, beside an interlacement of these categories, a characteristic complex of their own with further markings; see p. 63 below.) In addition, Spinoza represented an early Rationalistic, scientistic time-current. Vollenhoven clearly acknowledged that this designation does not fully circumscribe Spinoza's philosophy ("Spinoza" OE). In other writings, Vollenhoven noted that merely listing the type and the time-current of a conception amounts to the minimum of historical precision (1964a, 189; 1961c, 34).

In a certain sense, the sequence of the five categories concerns an orderly, systematic re-presentation.[53] When one actually studies the texts, the characteristics emerge in a diverging sequence. In contemporary parlance, the context of discovery is different from the context of justification.

Simplicity: A Mark of Truth?

According to these five criteria, Vollenhoven distinguished a large number of types, namely, nineteen main types and some thirty sub-types.[54] When one first encounters these, it seems difficult to understand such a considerable amount. Most studies in the history of philosophy make fewer distinctions. Vollenhoven (1938v) himself once tried it with the simple contrast between realism and nominalism, but this dilemma,

---

52. In *limited parallelism,* the parallel between the psychic and somatic aspects is limited, that is, atoms (matter) are not ensouled. They are ensouled, however, in *unlimited parallelism;* for instance, with the German evolutionist Haeckel (cf. his phrase *crystal souls,* in which the parallel runs without limitation, and his notion of God as "God-nature" or "Theophysis").

53. The sequence of Vollenhoven's five categories is somewhat relative. Averroës (Vollenhoven 1962, 37) and the Averroists follow the tradition of Aristotle's cosmological dualism (De Vogel 1958, 232). The Arabian philosopher adheres to the doctrine of the (universal) world soul (monopsychism), in which the individual (human being) participates. Immediately after dualism, the fifth category (E, partial universalism; cf. Figure 5 above) is to be considered.

54. 1962f. Cf. Bril 1986, 114–16, 171.

he found, did not do justice to the many distinctions a student encounters when studying philosophical concepts.[55]

In one sense, Vollenhoven can be interpreted as maintaining that types adhere either to a monistic or a dualistic origin (or, as we add, a pluralistic origin).[56] But he also clearly indicated that the dualism of Thomas Aquinas is something totally different from the dualism held by Descartes or by the neurologist Eccles. It is also fundamentally different from the dualistic view of the Cathari and the Manicheans.[57]

Things are more complicated than some would have us believe. The American psychologist Willis F. Overton, for example, distinguished only two types of "research traditions." Such a position is appealing and easy to grasp, as easy as when a teacher would say that the German language knows only two cases. Overton's simple scheme was rightly reproached by the Dutch psychologists C. Sanders and J. F. H. van Rappard: "[problems in this discussion] are the result of his classification of methodological positions which leave no room for other starting points" (1985, 294). Vollenhoven, in contrast, wished to gather each and every ontological starting point of the history of Western thought into his overview.

---

55. In a similar vein, A. P. Bos argued that Herman Dooyeweerd's view that Greek philosophy revolves around the polarity of matter and form cannot be maintained (1986; 1991a, 13–15).

56. Pluralism can possibly be associated with the Gnostic Cerinthus (c. A.D. 120) (cf. Wolfson 1956, 504–11; and Berkouwer 1954, 204–5). He was a contemporary of the martyr Polycarp, who labeled him an "enemy of the truth" (Rudolph 1987, 298).

    The christology of Rudolf Steiner (1861–1925) greatly resembles that of Cerinthus, though the latter is not mentioned (cf. Hemleben 1979, 35–37). At first, there were two "Jesus-boys," of whom the one acquired later the soul of the other (cf. the Kabbala, which also describes the notion that someone received the soul of another and thus acquired a second soul). In this way, the voice of Cerinthus resounds 1800 years later in the anthroposophic churches of the Steinerite Christian Community without apparently being recognized. Vollenhoven reckoned that Cerinthus and Steiner belong to the same type (1979a, 17; 1962f, 40). This is an interesting area for further study.

57. For instance, the dualism of Averroës (see note 53 on page 59) connects the soul with the world soul, in contrast to Thomistic dualism, which expressly rejects such a connection and opposes a dualism with a trichotomy, as, for instance, with the doctrine of the soul or the spirit as refined matter. Even within cosmogonic dualisms, there appeared a considerable difference between anthropological and andrological types (see page 50).

II. Typology

A. HOCKING: "TYPES AS CLUSTERS OF WORLDVIEWS"?

For Vollenhoven, it was a matter of principle to start his investigation at the roots of Western philosophy, namely, with the ancient Greeks. For it is the case that "one only really sees one's own time well to the degree that one sees it not as the beginning but (as it is in reality) as the conclusion of centuries of development in which the past speaks strongly, and which one denies at one's peril" (1961c, 33).

Cornelia de Vogel,[58] a contemporary of Vollenhoven, also noted fundamental typological traditions (1977, 95). "One can certainly say that during the eight to ten centuries of Greek thought that preceded, or were contemporaneous with, the formation of Christian dogmas, all types of philosophical thought were formed in their foundational appearances." Vollenhoven would completely concur with this remarkable statement of De Vogel, which was made two years after his last private lecture series.

What now exactly is a type and how can it be defined and traced historically? The American philosopher W. Ernest Hocking circumscribed it as follows: "Our beliefs tend to form clusters hanging from some significant stem-beliefs; such clusters we call types of philosophy" (1929, 20). He speaks here of clusters as metaphysical convictions along with differences in ethics, psychology, and esthetics. Vollenhoven's use of types has a similar aim: Thomism contains an entire complex of coherent themes; so does, as we saw, the andrological tradition, from *The Gospel of Thomas* to Weininger, via the Cathari. As Vollenhoven put it: "The investigation, adopted in this spirit, made me soon realize that every concept implies a multitude of themes" (1950e, 5). He did not desire to investigate the history of separate themes but wished to map these all out in their interconnectedness, analyzing "problem-patterns" (cf. p. 31 above). Thus, he did not strive after a "problem history" but for a *consequential* problem-historical method.

And yet, Hocking encountered problems with his definition, speaking as he did of naturalism and dualism, as well as of pragmatism and idealism as types. As a result, John Dewey's philosophy is reckoned to

---

58. Concerning the sad and, as I see it, unnecessary conflict between Professors De Vogel and Vollenhoven, see Popma 1952; Bril 1986, 182–83. In what follows we will see a remarkable correspondence between Vollenhoven's opinion and that of De Vogel.

belong to both the naturalistic (in the spirit of Charles Darwin [cf. Hart 1966]) and to the pragmatic "types." But then the understanding of a "belief" as constituting a cluster has been severely weakened. Vollenhoven reckoned pragmatism to belong to an entirely different category (time-current) than naturalism (type). Should one not wish to be a scatterbrain, one cannot honor simultaneously an original dualism and an original monism, though both standpoints are compatible with existentialism and pragmatism.[59]

Ambiguity can only lead to confusion. In this case, time-currents do not concern themselves with the structure of the cosmos, but pertain to normativeness, as Vollenhoven explained in his view of the place of the law (see Part Four below). Unlike Hocking's foundering definition of a type, Vollenhoven's definition distinguished between a cluster, "a multiplicity of themes," and a primarily ontological basic structure in the sense of the vertical structure of kingdoms.

These themes are connected with a relevant foundational structure. Parallelism cannot be united with creatianism; consistent evolutionism, which implies monism, is irreconcilable with dualism. For should the soul come from above, it cannot simultaneously originate by means of evolution.[60] Teleology, further, is incompatible with a monistic vitalism (Bergson); epiphenomenalism—the notion that consciousness is nothing more than an accompanying phenomenon of a somatic process—(Thomas Huxley) is compatible with materialism, but a "downward causation" (R. W. Sperry) cannot be united with this type. Thus, the ontological basic structure in the sense of the notion concerning the vertical structure of kingdoms is the fundamental category. It functions also as a magnet repelling certain themes and attracting others.

Vollenhoven never gave a general definition of a type. I venture to give the following description: "A type is an ontological basic structure, surrounded by a constellation of philosophical themes. Types are exclusive vis-à-vis one another and are more or less permanent in history."[61]

---

59. This pertains to "cross-divisions" (Centore 1979, 8) (cf. Hart's chart on page 31 and Figure 4 above). A certain animal can be both a bird and a resident of South America; it cannot be both a bird and a fish. A number can be even and be greater than the number ten, but it cannot simultaneously be an odd number. Centore emphasized this stricture for typological distinctions with one meaning.

60. See, e.g., Alfred Wallace (1823–1913) and the biologist David Lack (1957).

61. *Ontological basic structure* in the sense of the "vertical structures of kingdoms." *More or less permanent* is to be understood in connection with a transformation in a following time-current.

B. TYPOLOGICAL INVESTIGATION

When do we consider two philosophical systems to belong to the same type? Let us take, by way of an example, the historical trajectory of Spinoza's philosophy. In Marxist circles, there was a great interest in "Spinoza's deterministic worldview," while in other groups, he was viewed as a "humanistic and rationalistic freethinker." In nineteenth-century Germany, he was deemed the predecessor of pantheism (in the so-called "struggle concerning Spinozism"), but in the twentieth century, the religious-mystical side of his thinking was stressed.[62] So when did Vollenhoven reckon a thinker to belong to Spinozism in a typological sense? This happens when the ontology and the pattern of themes agree with each other. Spinozism is primarily the philosophy of identity: "One and the same essence presents itself, appearing in two attributes" (Eisler 1927, 708), but in later time-currents, within the same type, there are transformations as well.

In short, a typological investigation is *comparative cluster analysis*. As one investigates the history of philosophy, it appears that philosophers are being confronted by several basic problems that have been resolved in different ways. A typological investigation compares their responses to these basic problems.

Concerning *ontology*, there are the questions regarding the origin of human beings, of the world, and sometimes even of the world of the deities (e.g., in Gnosticism); the relationship between unity and multiplicity (monism, dualism); the connection between the ontic higher and lower (e.g., in anthropological interaction or parallelism); and that which is universal or individual. Ontology primarily concerns five categories as mentioned above (Figure 5) and discussed under the five headings (A-E above). This diversity of types, according to Vollenhoven (1961c, 15), goes back to "differences in the positing and answering of *problems*."

In addition to the first basic problem, that of ontology, the second basic problem (1959a, 43), to be treated in Part Four, focuses on the "*view of the place and the founding of the law*," that is, on the criteria and norms obtained—or on their absence, e.g., in relativism—from Plato to postmodernism. These *two main problems*—of ontology and the law—and their solutions, Vollenhoven analysed in several philosophical conceptions.

They are also posed and resolved by Vollenhoven himself (cf. p. 57 above). For instance, he rejected pantheistic and emanationistic monism,

---

62. See further Bril 1986, 176–77 (cf. 134–37, 147–49).

for there is a boundary between God and God's creation. He also rejected dualism, for instance, the Aristotelian view of the unmoved mover and the eternity of matter. After all: "In the beginning God created the heavens and the earth." He also rejected materialism, which holds that humans are mere matter, and animalism, which maintains that humans are nothing but a kind of ape. Vollenhoven also rejected the disqualification of both time and (as in Gnosticism) created matter.

Concerning each of these two basic problems, Vollenhoven attempted to articulate a Christian view, based on the words of the Psalmist (119:105): "Thy word is a lamp to my feet." In so doing, he developed a rather clear contrast between pagan, or synthetic, thought and a view developed by looking at the light shed by Holy Scripture (Tol 1993).

As one analyzes more deeply the various philosophical standpoints, one finds several historical responses. With the method of comparative cluster analysis, one discovers a network of relationships between these viewpoints. By investigating in this manner several concepts—not merely one question but, through an *integral* approach, a diversity of foundational problems—Vollenhoven strove to develop his so-called *consequential problem-historical method* (cf. 1950e, 5–6, 11; 1961c; Bril 1986, 178–81; and Tol 1993; 2003a).

I have explained Vollenhoven's method somewhat schematically. At times, one recognizes a representative of the same type through a constellation of elements found in that of an earlier conception (cf. p. 61 above). At times, a student who is only known for wholly agreeing with his teacher is reckoned to the same type. And sometimes, one lacks adequate data concerning a view to be able to formulate the answers to the named basic problems.

C. WHAT MOVED VOLLENHOVEN IN HIS INQUIRY?

Vollenhoven was certainly enamored of the history of philosophy as such, but that does not show the real motif of his tireless research. For historical inquiries are needed in order to understand the world of today. Vollenhoven wanted to help those seeking to acquire insight into the various philosophical backgrounds of, for instance, evolutionism or of several problems in physics and in theology. Even the tensions between several ecclesiastical denominations have more than once had a typological background. These can go back, via the age of the church fathers, to different phases of Platonic and Aristotelian philosophies (or to later

Aristotelian interpretations) and to poorly posed problems. Vollenhoven considered it his life's task to lay bare the historical connections of the problems of today.

Fiorenza and Metz wrote in *Mysterium salutis:*

> Within the Christian church there soon arose several anthropologies, of which some were more dualistic, others more monistic. But each time the leaders strove to conquer the problems originating from Greek thought with answers taken from the framework of Greek conceptions. (1968, 84)

Vollenhoven would be able to write the same as it concerns the problematics from that era which—when the necessary alterations have been made—have had their effect on through to the current thought.

Commenting on Vollenhoven's problem-historical method, Jacob Klapwijk wrote:

> Many had problems with the problem-historical method, though Vollenhoven—I must honestly concede—arrived at unheard-of discoveries using his uncommon method. He discovered a connection between Aristotle's later philosophy, the philosophy of Hellenism, and Monarchianism in the early Christian Church, a connection that might otherwise never have been noticed. (1978, 5)

What motivated Vollenhoven? He was convinced that a synthesis between biblical Christian and non-Christian philosophical themes was the cause of many difficulties, in church history as well.[63]

A continual study of the history of philosophy could clarify their background. While this history, with its many speculative systems, appeared to be very complicated, he tried to map out this complexity as carefully as possible. This was one reason Vollenhoven was considered complicated and difficult to understand. Nonetheless, when it pertained to the conviction of his own faith, he lived with a simplicity of heart (cf. Acts 2:46, "with glad and sincere hearts").

Vollenhoven was convinced that this kind of research would bring clarity in many areas—by pointing out a synthesis, for better under-

---

63. Within all types (and time-currents), rigorous synthetic conceptions at times appear to be possible—not only in the Scholastic tradition, but also in so-called anti-metaphysical (anti-Scholastic) thinking (e.g., in metaphysical materialism or in evolutionism).

  A synthetic approach also occurs in the mythologizing main group, for instance, in the Christian Gnosticism of the second century and in the modern Gnosticism of our own time, that is, in the churches of the Steinerite Christian Community with an anthroposophic orientation, and, further, the "Lectorium Rosicrucianum" among the rosicrucians and several directions within the present New Age movement. The synthesis will be discussed again below (p. 93).

standing the background of evolutionism, and for distinguishing philosophical directions in mathematics and in the natural sciences, as well as for daily life.

He saw his method as a possible means to elaborate on a Reformational philosophical view, which was also pertinent to the background of the special sciences. Therefore, he persisted in his labors, even after his retirement, until his powers became insufficient to sustain further research. From that time on, he lived only in a childlike trust in the Creator—his and ours alike.

PART FOUR

TIME-CURRENTS

I. The Struggle Concerning Method Continued

A study of successive time-currents—for instance, the long era from early Rationalism to our own age—confirms that each epoch favors a dominant view of science. I will highlight a few examples from the time-frame just mentioned.

During the epoch of Idealism, a very specific philosophy of nature prevailed, which in the biological inquiries of Johann Wolfgang von Goethe and others manifested itself in an idealistic morphology.[1] The multiformity of plants and animals was taken as merely a manifestation of unchanging, eternal original forms. Within the positivism that followed, one encountered totally different scientific ideals, especially the experimental and statistical methods. The fact that Charles Darwin waited twenty years (1839–1859) before publishing his thoughts about evolutionism (*The Origin of Species*) has something to do with it. For evolutionism had an entirely different background from idealistic morphology (cf. Bril 1993, 30–33).

Rationalism was succeeded, especially in Germany during the Weimar republic (1918–1933), by the philosophy of life, with its highly unique climate for the ideals of science.[2] Alongside of the Weimar academicians, the followers of Henri Bergson in France were known for their strongly antipositivistic approach, concerned as they were with "the method of inner experience" (*HWP* i, 832).

Older readers may still vividly remember existentialism, which stood for an ideal of science of its own, sometimes in alliance with phenomenology. It showed itself in the Netherlands, for instance, in the

---

1. Cf. Schierbeek 1944; and Bril 1986, 215f.
2. Cf. Radder 1982; Dolman 1984; also Bril 1986, 225f.

67

psychology and pedagogy of the Utrecht school. It is not accidental that in this period, the metabletic method arose and, here at least, acquired an especially large following. Particularly in his dissertation (1946), Jan Hendrik van den Berg, the originator of this method, was strongly influenced by the existentialism of Martin Heidegger and remained a defender of the phenomenological method (1989, 17). The existentialist climate manifested itself in America in the psychology of the third way, the so-called humanistic psychology.[3]

Let us next turn to neo-Marxism, whose strong dominance, also in the academic world, only recently diminished. This movement expressed itself not only in the sciences of sociology, economics, and politics but also in the sciences of history, biology, cultural anthropology, and theology. But that is now past tense. Nowadays, authors of publications or speakers at conferences do not wish to explain every aspect of human nature from the point of view of a class struggle or of a socioeconomic substructure; even if they think it to be true, they no longer do so.

At present, the new wave of poststructuralism and postmodernism is fast gaining in significance, making many inroads in the academic world as well. Other contemporary movements, like intertextualism, deconstructionism, and narrativism, also have a strong methodological tendency.

We conclude that many historical periods have their own criteria for science. Every period has implications for the "way of practicing science" (Gillespie 1979, 10). Likewise, according to Larry Laudan, every period has its "normative image of science":

> . . . every historical epoch exhibits one or more dominant, normative images of science. . . . *Every* practicing scientist, past and present, adheres to certain views about how sciences should be performed, about what counts as an adequate explanation. . . . *These norms . . . have been perhaps the single major source for most of the controversies in the history of science. . . .*[4]

So too, Van den Berg's metabletic method and Foucault's structuralism pointed explicitly to the specific historical implications for the sciences of a certain epoch.

---

3. Translator's note: "In the early 1960s, a group of psychologists headed by Abraham Maslow started a movement referred to as third-force psychology. These psychologists claimed that the other two forces in psychology, behaviorism and psychoanalysis, neglected a number of important human attributes" (Hergenhahn 1997, 529).

4. Laudan 1977, 58. Van der Steen, discussing "methodological norms," wrote, "Methodology is an essential part of science, having a normative character" (1991, 125).

When Vollenhoven stated that the time-currents concern the place of the law, he did not explicitly mention the scientific criteria for a period. But "normative images of science" as a datum completely concur with his views and are implicitly included in these.

Vollenhoven's view concerning the background of the problematics of time-currents extends much further, however. It touches a continual process in the history of Western Europe that starts with the ancients and is still active in contemporary thought.

II. From Plato to Descartes

Time-currents are succeeded by newer versions, and these, in turn, are swept aside by still others. Do time-currents have a characteristic of their own? What is the core of the problem?

When we discussed the colors of a rose in Part One, I mentioned the process of the interiorization or a priorizing of the secondary qualities (since Galileo in 1623). Something similar happened to feelings and spirituality. The distance between humans and the (external) world became greater. Some spoke of a split between subject and object. Van den Berg called it an "ill-fated separation" (1956, 249). According to Delfgaauw, alienation grew: ". . . humans alienated themselves from reality, from themselves, and from the world" (1989, 27). Vollenhoven referred to the same process.

Is the core of the process of interiorization located in the split between subject and object, as we just mentioned? We believe that the essence of this process has remained outside of the discussion. For it concerns questions regarding human autonomy. What are the possibilities of thinking? Are autonomous persons able to acquire certainty, to reveal truth through their own strength, without divine revelation? From where does one draw—be it in ethics or in jurisprudence—when it comes to the norm for good and evil? Are these norms contained in human reason? If this is not the case, are there then rational methods to discover these? Or must one simply conclude that all is a chimera, that there are thus no permanent norms? Does the historian rightly speak of a relativistic historicism?

This complex of questions appears to be related to a progressive historical process, of which early Rationalism—the Enlightenment—

constitutes a remarkable phase. The Dutch historian Jan Romein expressed it in the following striking words (1971, 505): "As a single free spirit dared in the sixteenth century to leave the final decision up to one's own conscience, so the Enlightenment moved the *authority from the outside to the inside: human reason becomes the new and the last authority*" (italics mine).

How did this development start and how did it continue? That will be the subject of this part of the history of the theme of the a priori: the history of autonomous human beings, from Plato to present-day Irrationalism.

The Process of Interiorization: From Plato to Descartes

I shall attempt to explore the history of the theme of the a priori from Plato to Descartes and later thinkers, aware that Vollenhoven himself did not publish a summary of it.

We commence with Plato. In his younger years, Athens' political situation was dismal. In 399 B.C., his teacher Socrates was condemned to death, and at that time the Sophists preached moral relativism, thereby undercutting the validity of traditional norms. Many Sophists maintained that there was no official standard. Should it not be clear who was in the right, the issue became how one could move in that direction. The same approach was used regarding questions about good and evil. As a result, the art of reasoning in the hands of the Sophists became more a means of persuasion than of conviction, for, according to them, there was no objectively binding moral law in the realm of ethics.[5]

In opposing relativism, Plato searched for absolute ethical norms, for "justice in itself," independent of factual human behavior. It was not for nothing that Plato portrayed his teacher Socrates as an opponent of the Sophists (De Vogel 1967, 217). He viewed this problem in relation to other areas of philosophy—epistemology (namely, how to acquire knowledge of norms), logic, and ontology (Runia 1991). He did not see any ultimate answer in reference to the visible world but pointed beyond it to an intelligible realm that only thinking minds could inspect. In this intelligible realm, in the background world, there were, alongside of the ideas, also the perfect examples of what are, for us, imperfect mathematical objects, such as our imperfect circles—namely, pure roundness and the pure triangle.[6] Plato reasoned as follows: "Because the things perceived, as we say, can never be fully known as they really are (beauti-

---

5. Störig 1959, 138 (cf. De Strijcker 1980, 62).
6. Runia 1991 (cf. De Vries 1957).

ful, equal or just), and because the pronouncement 'this is beautiful' must be capable of being true, we must accept imperceptible realities, ideas, 'in addition' to things perceived. Thus, ideas, as ideal forms, are what things themselves fully are: perfect, nothing but beautiful, equal, and just."[7]

Vollenhoven wrote about Plato that beginning with his so-called middle dialogues, Plato proceeds to

> . . . search for the law outside of the cosmos, "outside" (Gk. *choris*) signifying here (according to the drawing in his *Politeia*) "behind." Behind the true, the beautiful, and the good within the cosmos, he now adopts, namely, the existence of truth itself, beauty itself, and goodness itself. In addition to these "ideas," also the plani-metric examples of the stereo-metric figures are under the jurisdiction of the background of becoming. . . . One can perceive the background only with the mind (Gk. *nous*); from an epistemological viewpoint it is called intelligible (Gk. *noeton*). ("Plato" in *OE*)

Interestingly enough, De Vogel made statements that are clearly similar to Vollenhoven's view. She entertained the question "whether our moral concepts and judgments are rooted . . . in a transcendent reality" or whether one rejects that view and posits that humans create values. According to De Vogel:

> This problem dates to the fifth century B.C., to the time of the so-called Sophists. Plato places Socrates over against them, permitting him to defend across the entire spectrum that there is *a transcendent reality;* that moral concepts and judgments are valid, not only in our world, but also in the world-to-come; not only among humans, but also for the deities; and that nothing is as important for humans as to live in accord with those *principles, which as a solid, immovable order are above them.* (1967, 124; italics mine)

De Vogel called Plato's doctrine of the ideas an "ethical metaphysics" (ibid., 217).[8]

---

7. This concise and clear formulation is derived from Berger 1992, 206.
8. Cf. De Vries 1957, 12–13, 15. A similar interpretation is found in Wytzes. This former professor of classics in Kampen wrote: "Plato is to be forever honored and greatly esteemed for lending the norms such an elevated (too lofty, indeed) and absolutely valid character" (1960, 14). "Plato discerned that humans are not the measuring rod for all things, but that there is a divine norm (we would say, the Law of God) which demands obedience from us" (cf. Zwaan 1973, 200).
   Vollenhoven's view is not entirely identical to this description (cf. 1950e, 26; 1956b, 14). He had reservations about Plato, particularly in connection with the law (cf. 1956b, 2; 1961c, 12; 1963a, 128). They had to do with the commandment of love and religious direction (cf. Matthew 22:34–40), i.e., with Vollenhoven's own religious conviction and systematic philosophy.

Skepticism within the Academy and Plotinus's Solution

Following Plato's death, a period of doubt emerged, also in Plato's own Academy. At first, the skeptics, as they were called, doubted that the ideas could be known, later that these actually existed. Following the skeptical period, there emerged the notion of the a priori: the ideas, the laws, and the norms do exist, either in the divine macro-cosmos or in the human micro-cosmos. Cicero (106–43 B.C.) used the term *reason* (Lat. *ratio*), that is, the human intellect equipped with a priori concepts. These are the roots of Rationalism, commencing with Descartes (c. 1600).

Hart, who studied under Vollenhoven, summarized the development after Plato as follows:

> . . . the denial of conditional structures gave rise to a practical crisis. Practical life had been robbed of its necessary certainties, its points of orientation, its criteria for judging correctly in practical affairs. . . . The final answer came in the spirit of the epistemological attitude: certainty lay in the inborn presuppositions of the understanding, in universals preceding experience but determinative of it. The universally valid conditions for all experience were located in the universally valid logical concepts of the individual human mind or the divine mind or the universal mind. (1966, 2)

Plotinus (c. A.D. 250) adopted this approach such that "the ideas became the original thoughts of the deity" (*HWP* iv, 61). But he also modified it. For it would be inconsistent for him to place all the ideas in the One (Gk. *to hen*),[9] as in that case the One would no longer be "One," or pure unity. "Therefore, the Mind (Gk. *nous*) is the place of the ideas for Plotinus" (*HWP* iv, 61).

Less than two hundred years later (c. 385), Augustine concurred in many respects with the teachings of the neo-Platonists, espousing as he did a "Christian neo-Platonism." He too believed that the Platonic ideas were found in the divine mind (*HWP* iv, 63).

Afterward there appeared a long road, a progressive process of interiorization, from Augustine to Descartes.

From the Stoics to Descartes

Can it be said, indeed, that we can draw an historical line from the Stoic notion of innate concepts to Descartes, who more than once spoke of ideas? He held to ideas acquired through experience as well as

---

9. He held to a negative theology: the transcendent deity is neither this nor that (cf. *Dictionary of the History of Ideas* III, 372b).

to innate ideas (Lat. *ideae innatae*).[10] Is there then a relation between Descartes' views and the process signaled beforehand?

Vollenhoven, whose interpretation I shall mention first, noted concerning Descartes: "Only the a priori concepts, the innate ideas with practical significance (and especially arithmetic truths which possess scientific significance) are really solid. Both, however, are concepts and judgments . . . the property of the thinking mind" (1956b, 34). From the context, it is clear that Vollenhoven saw a direct relationship between René Descartes and the earlier history of the theme of a priori.

Others agree. William of Ockham, for example, initiated a development in which the ideas are moved from the divine intellect to human subjectivity—a development, we read, "characterized by a gradual loosening of the ideas from the divine intellect and which makes possible a shift in the idea-model to the subjectivity of human thinking," a notion held by Descartes (*HWP* iv, 101). In another study about innate ideas, Brandt (1977) pointed out that Cicero was the first to use this terminology, a tradition on which Descartes was dependent (*HWP* iv, 55, 103–5). Here as well, De Vogel held a similar view: "A line can be drawn from the Stoic doctrine of innate concepts to Descartes" (1950, 185).

A First Schematic Glance Back

In the seventeenth century, John Locke and those like him stated that the fragrant red rose, in fact, consisted merely of bare primary qualities (like extension). The world in front of and behind the eye was interpreted differently from the previous eras—as presented in schema earlier (p. 19).

As Vollenhoven and others explained, the notion of the a priori was found much earlier.[11] I can now expand the first figure.

---

10. Translator's note: Actually, Descartes knows three kinds of ideas (cf. *Meditations of First Philosophy*, Meditation 3): "But among these ideas, some appear to me to be innate, others adventitious, and others to be made by myself (factitious). . . ."

11. Regarding reincarnation and the use of the term *a priori:* The term *a priori* is found for the first time in Ockham's writings (c. 1300); using it in regards to antiquity is somewhat arbitrary.
    Plato favored the doctrine of reincarnation (Solmsen 1983). One can possess knowledge of the ideas even without any experience of them in this life. This knowledge can be designated terminologically as "a priori knowledge" (cf. De Vries [1957, 14, 53], agreeing with N. Hartmann [1935]). But in that case, too, intelligibility is actually located outside of the human mind. De Vries also pointed out that Aristotle permits "the idea of roundness to be 'in' the thing" (14), whereas Plato rejects the notion that the idea is "in" the soul.

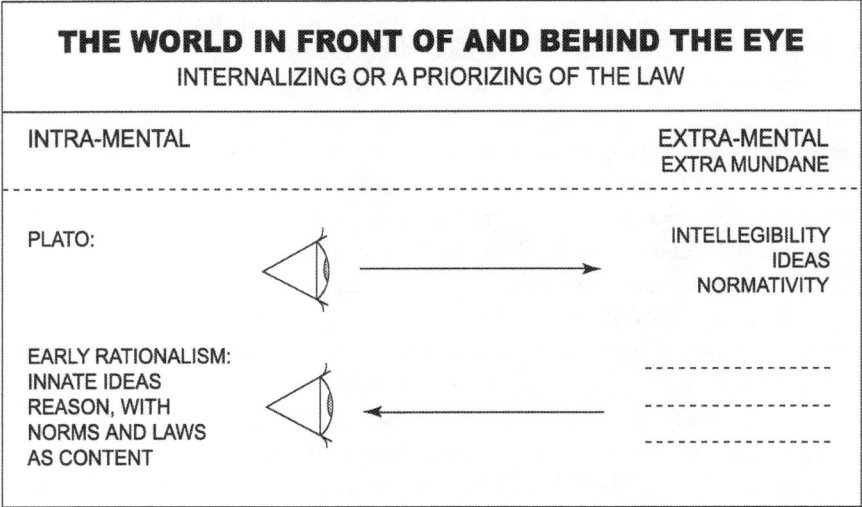

Figure 6. The history of the theme of a priori to Positivism

III. The Period of Early Rationalism: From Its Growth to Its Decay

A. VOLLENHOVEN'S INTRODUCTION

The time-currents of Rationalism cover about three hundred years (c. 1600–1900). Vollenhoven summarized the Age of Rationalism as follows:

> The term "rationalism" means the over-estimation of Ratio but what does Ratio mean? *Ratio is "Reason,"* i.e., *the intellect equipped with a priori's.* "Ratio" is therefore a left conception. It shows a lack of perception if one accepts the problematic, "What is the relationship between faith and reason?" God has given man not Reason but intellect and left thought has first made intellect into Reason. Reason is therefore no more than the product of an illusion but of a productive one. For there has been a time when many who cherished this illusion believed in Reason.
>
> The period during which the intellect equipped with a priori's was the foundational concept of West European thought, covered around 1600–1900.
>
> The concept "Reason" itself was much older, as we have seen. One finds this concept already with Cicero who, because he was no original thinker of note, had undoubtedly borrowed this term from Greek philosophy that had known the a priori theme since around 300 B.C. Since that time, this theme

had made steady progress. Historically speaking, therefore, rationalism did not come into being spontaneously. But what gave this theme pre-dominance around 1600?

The looked-for occurrence was the *displacement of the psychic object functions to the spirit or the observing of the knower*. This a priori, preceded by that of the logical object near the end of the Middle Ages, was the work of *Galileo*, an Italian representative of parallelism with atomism.

The a priori theme made much progress here. Even qualities such as scent, sound and color now belonged to the inventory of the knower, according to this current that soon dominated. Hereby these qualities were denied to the knowable, however, and the way became open to a development that, because of the approach to the knowable by the then-current theory of knowledge, resulted in philosophers identifying physical things with "matter," i.e., with something that as yet only possessed "*primary qualities*," a terminology that very clearly betrays its subjectivistic origin. Even the difference between subject functions and qualities was lost sight of!

Rationalism has also had its history. One understands this best—seeing the character of this period—with the help of some distinctions from the theory of knowledge. The most important of these is that of thinking activity and thought-result or knowledge-content. Now, that content encompasses not only experiential concepts, according to the rationalist, but also the a priori concepts and a priori judgments that constitute experience. That is why rationalism, because of its pre-history, initially strongly emphasized that which we call the result. This Old Rationalism, barring some exceptions, dominated the situation until around 1830. During 1831 Hegel dies; he was one of the greatest of the old current in this Old Rationalism. But something new emerges, namely, in 1830 the stress begins to be laid on the activity of reason rather than its content. Also there are a priori's. These bear an active character, however; one goes to work on the knowable with a priori *methods*. This conception typifies the late or young rationalism.[12]

Let us next follow Vollenhoven's description of Early Rationalism (circa 1600–1830).

During these centuries, one can distinguish another three currents. Initially, it was reason that was raved about, the scientific. This conception ultimately only made sense as long as one greatly over-estimated scientific knowledge. Eventually, however, also the Old Rationalists realized that reason was not only scientific but that such a thing as non-scientific knowledge also existed which they then understood as non-scientific reason. Hence, we get the phi-

---

12. 1956b, 33–34. For Vollenhoven, the adjective *leftist* (in the sentence, "Ratio is . . . a left conception") signified a biblical, not a political notation (cf. "to the left," at Ecclesiastes 10:2 [cf. *RGG* 4, 382]). The Latin adjective *sinister*, or *left*, had an unfavorable connotation. Concerning one's personal attitude toward the commandment of love (Matthew 22:34–40), Vollenhoven spoke of *direction* (1963a, 128) and in this connection also of "left" and "right" (1961c, 9, 12; 1963b, 11).

losophy of the Enlightenment (*Aufklärung*), or practicalism, forming the second current. Gradually a fierce battle arose between scientialism—the technical term for over-estimation of scientific reason—and practicalism; it then becomes necessary to think of a reconciliation. Thus, the time had come for Old Idealism that connected scientialism and practicalism.

A. Scientialism

This current dominates during the time of the "Great Systems." Apart from Galileo, Spinoza, Leibniz and Newton also belonged to it but so also did John Locke and Berkeley.

Descartes is the man of anthropological interaction theory. He accepts the macro- micro-cosmos theme and speaks of god as infinite and of people as finite. Principally knowing-theory minded, he struggles here with the problem of how we come to the concept of the infinite. He answers himself, "This must have been given to us, particularly arithmetical truths that possess scientialistic significance." But both are concepts and judgments. Naturally, they do not float loosely in the world; they belong to the thinking spirit. Hence, the well-known, *Cogito, ergo sum*, i.e., "I think, therefore I am." But the main thing for Descartes is the innate idea and arithmetical truth, not the spirit that possesses these two. Sometimes that was postulated later by Late Rationalistic interpretation, but a priori conceptions and judgments are in the foreground. (ibid., 34)

Thus far Vollenhoven's own words.

Innate Ideas

Do the a priori ideas (the innate ideas) found in Rationalism and held by Descartes have the character of a law? In Plato's philosophy, the ideas had a normative character (see p. 69). John Nelson pointed out that the theory of the innate ideas "claims that *all morally right judgment* or all science, or both, rest upon or consist in a knowledge *a priori* either of (a) *universal principles governing reality* or (b) objects transcending sensory experience" (1967, 196; ital. mine). This definition of innate ideas indicates not only a normative component but also posits a relation with the concept of "a priori." Even René Descartes appeared to speak expressly of a priori laws when he boldly remarked in the *Discourse* that

I have also observed *certain laws* which God has so established in Nature, and of which He has imprinted *such ideas on our minds*, that, after having reflected sufficiently upon the matter, we cannot doubt their being accurately observed in all that exists or is done in the world. (I, 106; ital. mine)

Descartes wrote about "certain laws . . . imprinted . . . on our minds." When Vollenhoven remarked that the theme of a priori is important for time-currents, then one can rightly say that they "primarily concern questions surrounding the place of the law" (1961c, 15).

B. Early Manifestations

How did Rationalism manifest itself and how did it develop? We begin with early Rationalism, which is divided into three periods. As we saw before, Vollenhoven distinguished between scientialism (e.g., Descartes and others), the Enlightenment (e.g., Rousseau), and Idealism (e.g., Kant and Fichte), respectively.[13] We will review a few examples from each period, first from the disciplines of theology and ethics and then from the natural sciences and political studies.

Theology and Ethics

(a) Scientialism. In the days of Descartes, during the period of the great systems, the English philosopher Herbert of Cherbury (1583–1648) developed a new theology according to which humans did not need divine revelation—for all human knowledge rested on "common notions" (Lat. *notitiae communes*) that are immediately evident to everyone. Thus, when it comes to religion, reason (*ratio*) has autonomous sway. He sharply criticized faith in revelation and "the Christian doctrine of divine grace, of which humans, as he saw it, had no need."[14] He is sometimes called the "father of English deism" (Mossner 1967). Later, though taking his start from deism, Darwin, in the end as a positivist, embraced a totally different theology.

Such strong pronouncements are hard to find in Dutch theology of that period. In the Netherlands, Rationalistic theology was at first the theology of old liberalism (cf. Roessingh 1914, 7–25). Van der Willigen, for example, wrote about "reasonable religion," about an "open training in practicing true virtue," and about a religion based on "proper conduct" (19). Jesus was praised for his "honesty," "sense of duty," and "steady character" (21).

Let us listen to J. H. van der Palm (1763–1840), first a preacher and then a professor in the city of Leiden. In his *Salomo* (1822), he wrote:

> What a lovely torch is the light of reason, a torch lit by God himself within our most inner being. . . . Therefore, we have something divine in us. . . . [O]ur reasonable mind . . . causes us to approach the nature of the deity, who is the highest, the most perfect reason.[15]

---

13. Vollenhoven discussed the period of early Rationalism in 1964a (189–92) as well.
14. Sassen 1946, 243 (cf. Vollenhoven 1959f, "Herbert van Cherbury" in *OE*).
15. According to Oosterhoff 1981, 23; cf. 22, 24.

Roessingh reckoned Van der Palm to belong to the period of old liberalism, which differs from the more Enlightenment-oriented Groningen School and has absolutely no feeling for the third phase, the Idealism of Kant, Fichte, and Schelling.[16] Van der Palm spoke of "new castles built in the air, founded on barbaric admiration" and of a "kind of philosophical fanaticism, hatched in dismayed German brains" (so Roessingh 1914, 24).

(b) The Enlightenment. Meanwhile, at least in philosophy, the intellectual climate had changed. In the new time-current, the Enlightenment, one-sided scientialism was resisted. Practical life and certainly feelings needed more attention than they were getting—think of Rousseau's religion of sentiment (1956b, 35–36; 1964a, 191).

Anthony Shaftesbury developed an ethics in the spirit of the Enlightenment. Sassen described his view, in which

> humans have an innate ability to make moral distinctions, a moral sense, . . . by virtue of which we, for every reasonable value judgment, through spontaneous approval or disapproval mark an act as morally good or bad. . . . An independent ethics according to reasonable insight, as he had put together, appears as certain to Shaftesbury as mathematics, on the basis of inner experience. . . .[17]

As noted earlier, *inward* was Shaftesbury's favorite adjective (Romein 1971, 439).

The Dutch theologians followed this development of "inwardness" and feelings carefully, albeit rather late. Hofstede de Groot, for example, is a well-known figure of the Groningen School, who disliked scientistic Rationalism and the theology of the old liberals mentioned above. Roessingh reported that "the members of the Groningen school were very resolute in finding . . . the essence of religion to reside in feeling"; citing De Groot: ". . . unshakable and certain is only that which rests on personal convictions of the heart, on one's emotional life, on inner experience" (1926 i, 31). Roessingh noted especially the influence of the Germans Herder and Jacobi and the Dutchman Hemsterhuis, who are familiar Enlightenment figures.

A few years ago, in a dissertation devoted to the "Groningen Divines," J. Vree, likewise, pointed at the influence of Hemsterhuis, Jacobi, Herder, and Van Heusde: "The influence that extends from all these people I summarize in words of feeling and especially, with Herder, of

---

16. It was especially the theology and the spiritual mentality of the old liberals against which the Secession (Hendrik de Cock and others) turned (Vree 1984, 30–61; cf. De Wolff 1954).

17. Sassen 1946, 243f. Cf. Vollenhoven "Shaftesbury" in *OE*; also Sprague 1967.

history" (1984, 338; cf. 334, 348). Feelings, according to Vollenhoven as well, was a marked feature of the Enlightenment.[18]

(c) Idealism. Early Rationalism reached its climax in the following period, namely, in philosophical Idealism, which, according to Vollenhoven, attempted to "lift the tension between scientism and the Enlightenment by rendering justice to both epistemological viewpoints" ("Rationalism" *OE*).

Kant, the father of Idealism, had an incalculable impact on Western thought. With him, the human subject becomes autonomous in a loaded sense: the laws of nature originate in theoretical reason, the laws for reasonable acting in practical reason (Geertsema 1980, 314). Trusting in reason is the leading motif, which "above all is an objective authority to which one can appeal as the inner light, present in principle in every human being" (Kuypers 1966, 121). Here is the foundation of autonomy, namely, "making reason the law unto oneself" (G. *Selbstgesetzgebung durch Vernunft*). In his *Critique of Practical Reason,* Immanuel Kant wrote, "The *autonomy* of the will is the sole principle of all moral laws and of the duties conforming to them; *heteronomy* of [arbitrary] choice, on the other hand, . . . is opposed . . . to the morality of the will."[19] What is heteronomy? Imposed authority, coming to humans from the outside—as do the instructions of Scripture.[20]

Vollenhoven wrote about Kant: "Humans must consider themselves reasonable, moral beings—free and autonomous—prescribing for themselves through reason the lawfulness of their actions" ("Kant" *OE*). In the concluding paragraph of his *Critique of Practical Reason,* Kant noted, "Two things fill the mind with ever new and increasing admiration and awe . . . the starry heavens above me and the moral law within me" (1956, 166). *Within me*—Plato's intelligible world, once outside of humans, on the other side of the cosmos, is now found inside of them. One is again reminded of Vollenhoven's statement that time-currents concern especially the place of the law.

One might think that Herman Dooyeweerd has an altogether different view of Rationalism.[21] Yet, one finds with him pronouncements akin

---

18. Some use the term *Enlightenment* in a broader sense, for instance, when referring to early Rationalism. Vollenhoven, like Ueberweg, used it in a restricted sense.

19. Kant 1956, 33 (cf. *HWP* i, 707).

20. Several critics note that we must distinguish between autonomy, heteronomy, and theonomy—subjection to the norm of God's law. *HWP* i, 714f.; "Autonomie" in *Christelijke encyclopaedie*, 398.

21. Translator's note: In contrast to Vollenhoven, Dooyeweerd treated the entire history of philosophy by means of four ground motifs (cf. Bril 1995; Vunderink 2000).

to Vollenhoven's view as explained above. For instance, in 1941 he wrote: ". . . the dogma of the autonomy of 'Reason' compels, however, critical immanence philosophy to elevate the transcendental thinking subject to lawgiver. In this way the mark of 'general validity' is pressed on the subjective a priori, which, in truth, is due merely to the structural law of thought" (1941, 14).

At this point, the question can be raised of whether the mentality of a time-current is unavoidable. In the Rationalistic era, neither reason (Lat. *ratio*) nor the origin of reason was subject to discussion (Thévenaz 1960). The mentality of a time-current has a very compelling character—is a mega-trend, one could say. Can one resist it? Michel Foucault emphasized that individuals have no independent significance, that they are replaceable in the system of relationships (Bakker 1973, 17, 65, 135).

And yet, criticism has consistently been voiced. Friedrich Jacobi, a contemporary of Immanuel Kant, interpreted the latter's autonomous ethics as "self-divinization" (G. *Selbstgötterei; HWP* i, 711). Later, Isaac da Costa, some fifty years his junior, wrote in his *Bezwaren tegen de Geest der Eeuw* ("Objections against the Spirit of the Century"): "We have Kant's proud teaching that humans are their own lawgiver" (1974 edition, 14). Still later, Brummelkamp, one of the leaders in the Secession (Dutch *Afscheiding*) noted that "the teaching of virtue and good works, one's own decency, and the excellence of humans and of Reason, all these were the deities, with whose praise one could not be satisfied."[22] *The deities*—concerning that period Jan Romein, too, spoke of human reason as the final authority.

"The enlightened and more developed part of the nation," as they called themselves, judged these critics to be narrow-minded. Contemporary postmodernism is inclined to agree with the critique against Rationalism given by each of these three men.[23]

The Sciences

Thus far, I have discussed philosophy, theology, and ethics during the period of early Rationalism. But we can encounter a similar Rationalism in politics, physics, and biology as well.

---

22. Namely, liberalism (see p. 77 above). Oosterhoff 1981, 24—citing J. A. Wormser, *Het leven van Simon van Velzen* (1916, 85).

23. This critique partly corresponds to the approach of Zuidema, who was brave enough to go against fashionable Existentialism (1948) and against Marxism (1957).

Vollenhoven noted that, when it came to the knowledge of reason, the Enlightenment was particularly interested in knowledge of a practical nature ("Rationalisme" *OE*). Jean-Jacques Rousseau, who knew all about "the knowledge of practical reason," dealt with the nature of the state and the state of nature. Near the beginning of his *Discourse on the Origin of Inequality*, written in 1755, he wrote the following remarkable passage: "Let us therefore begin by putting aside all the facts, for they have no bearing on the question" (1992, 17). He did not say: "Let us look first at all the facts," but "let us put all the facts to the side." Why? Because the existing historical data do not matter. "The state of nature must be constructed by means of reason, aided therein by imagination."[24] It would seem that the state of nature is a fact constructed by Rousseau's reason.

The Swiss biologist and philosopher Charles Bonnet (1720–93) had a high regard for reason. In his view of embryology, he honored, but in extreme form, the notion of preformation, as did Malebranche, who lived a few years before him. Every generation is hidden in an "egg cell" of the previous generation, like a box in a box, on back to creation. Bonnet views this notion of preformation, or the theory of encapsulation, as a triumph of pure reason. In his own words, "This hypothesis of encapsulation is one of the most beautiful victories that pure understanding has gained over the senses."[25]

A century earlier, René Descartes conceded, "Should experience show that light needs time to travel, then my entire philosophy would collapse" (so Hooykaas 1976, 149). "The natural sciences cause everything to unfold a priori," according to Schelling, while Fichte claimed that even nature is a "positing" of the "absolute Ego."[26]

But human reason seems to err continually. Later on, such Rationalistic physics and biology proved to be unsustainable. In the end, a revision of the foundations of early Rationalism could not be avoided. And so Jacobi, Kant's critic, was placed in the right.

The problematics concerning the inside and the outside, the history of the theme of a priori, continued in the course of philosophy, showing the approaching decline of early Rationalism and the ascent of positivism.

---

24. Lemaire 1980, 51.
25. Gould 1977, 21 (citing Bonnet *Contemplation de la nature,* 1964, 162f.).
26. Walgrave 1981, 538; cf. *HWP* i, 470.

IV. Late Rationalism: Reason as Instrument

In late Rationalism, Vollenhoven again distinguished three periods: positivism (1830–c. 1850, e.g., Auguste Comte and John Stuart Mill), neo-Enlightenment[27] (e.g., among others, Eucken and Dühring), and neo-Idealism (1870–1900/1920, e.g., the neo-Kantian schools of Marburg and Baden, distinguishable according to typological differences).[28]

I will limit myself to positivism and neo-Idealism (the first and third movements within late Rationalism) and to one representative from these two broad currents of thought.

A. POSITIVISM

Several studies designate 1831, the year of Hegel's death, as marking the end of the preceding period of early Idealism. Within four years, Wolfgang von Goethe, Friedrich Schleiermacher, and Wilhelm von Humboldt would also die. Then positivism commenced with its drastic changes. Emile Littré (1801–1881) is a case in point. He was a French physician, a man of letters, a philosopher, and an ardent supporter of positivism. As far as he was concerned, the content of morality is not innate: "morality is innate, its content is acquired."[29] Moral sensibility is a human organ and belongs to us by nature; whereas the content of morality is an alternating, relative acquisition.[30] In other words, values are time-bound and no longer holding a priori.

First, I shall give Vollenhoven's circumscription of neo-Rationalism before we hear the voice of one positivist.

According to Vollenhoven, early Rationalism accepted that reason (Lat. *ratio*) had laws and norms as its contents. Neo-Rationalism, however, "no longer approaches reason as *content* but as *activity*: the rational a priori's are no longer concepts and judgments, but methods of investigation and approach" (1964a, 192). Reason becomes an ability, a path to follow, an instrument—rather than content (1956b, 33).

This deeply moving view showed up in the positivism of the mature Darwin. Human reason arises given its survival value. But can we trust it

---

27. This term represents Vollenhoven's intention better than "neopositivism"; cf. 1982a, 76, 93.
28. Delfgaauw (1952) simply designated this period as Idealism, as does Sassen-Delfgaauw (1957).
29. "*Le moral* [morality] *est inné, la morale* [the content of morality] *est acquise.*"
30. According to Banning 1965, 18.

when it comes to the question of good and evil, to the fundamental questions of life? Darwin had his doubts about it. In his own words, "With me the horrid doubt always arises whether the convictions of men's mind, which has been developed from the minds of lower animals, are of any value or are at all trustworthy?"[31] Darwin was a man of integrity in admitting some awful doubts about the reliability of reason and the content of reason. Ernst Haeckel was a bit more foolhardy.

There is good reason to take Darwin's question seriously (Lack 1957, 104). Doubt would continue to haunt philosophy like an evil spirit.

Positivism and Darwin's Theology

Few realize any longer that Darwin completed his theological studies and received his B.A. degree at Cambridge the same year his journey around the world on the S.S. *Beagle* commenced—1831. According to his autobiography, he found the works of the Anglican theologian William Paley, which he read as a student, interesting. Paley (1743–1805) was a protagonist of a Rationalistic natural theology.[32] In his famous *Natural Theology* (1802), he endeavored to prove the existence of God by means of the purposefulness of nature (the so-called argument from design). At first, Darwin was very much taken in by Paley's discussions about plant and animal adaptation. "I was charmed and convinced by the long line of argumentation," so he wrote in his autobiography. After a while, however, he rejected this idea. Nature's purposefulness does not prove a designer; rather, it is the result of natural selection. In fact, "without natural selection you cannot solve Paley's problem."[33]

Initially, Charles Darwin was a Unitarian, not an Anglican, as was his highly respected wife Emma Wedgwood. Later on, his faith disappeared more and more. Yet, he did not call himself an atheist but an agnostic,

---

31. Darwin 1887, I, 316; cf. Lack 1957, 4, 101, 104.
32. "Paley" in *OE*. Cf. Sprague 1967.
33. Popper 1978, 345—citing Darwin 1887, III, 158f. I would note that one does not become a Christian through a theoretical proof of God's existence. For in that case, one would place one's deepest trust in one's own intellect instead of in Christ who proclaims, "no one comes to the Father, but by me" (John 14:6).

    Viewing adaptations as "design" is not the cause of faith; rather, in faith we can discern design in nature. *The Belgic Confession* of Guido de Bres reads: "We know [God] by two means" (Article 2). But the pronoun *we* must not be read as "we, humans," but as "we, believers" (Van Genderen and Velema 1992, 59; cf. Berkouwer 1955, Chapter 10). On the other hand, Psalm 148, for example, speaks of "stormy wind fulfilling his command!" In *Wending* 17 (1962) 5/6, "design" is not mentioned, but "the bitter riddle of the good creation" is referred to (265f.).

that is, one for whom it is impossible to know anything about God's existence. In a letter dated 1879, he wrote: "In my most extreme fluctuations I have never been an atheist [I think] . . . but not always that an Agnostic would be the more correct description of my state of mind."[34] Reason cannot prove the existence of God, according to Darwin. "One might as well try to illuminate the midnight sky with the candle as to throw light on metaphysics" (Desmond and Moore 1991, 634).

In Darwin, we enter a totally different climate of thought than the one weathered by his countryman, Herbert of Cherbury, who espoused an early Rationalistic natural theology grounded in "common notions." Cherbury, according to Vollenhoven, was working with *ratio* and contentful concepts. The positivists, in contrast, by rejecting these, limited themselves to reason as a method.

In 1881, two avowed atheists visited Darwin: Ludwig Büchner and the dubious Edward Aveling.[35] Although he could not agree with their atheism, he could agree on one subject, namely, that Christianity was "not supported by evidence" (Desmond and Moore 1991, 658).

The term *agnosticism,* introduced by the militant Thomas Huxley, Darwin's close associate, appeared surprisingly compatible with the positivistic turn within Rationalism. Paley's teleological proof for the existence of God failed, and the innate ideas, including those of the father of deism, "vanished" in positivism—there being *no evidence.* Agnosticism was the positivistic continuation of the deism of early Rationalism.[36]

Van den Berg, following Gilson, dismissively characterized positivism (at the time of Darwin) as intellectual asceticism.[37] This may be true, but the period that preceded it was one of intellectual boastfulness.

B. NEO-IDEALISM

The successive periods of neo-Enlightenment and neo-Idealism followed on the heels of a sober-minded and coldhearted positivism.

From the neo-Idealists, I select the gifted and fascinating Leiden theologian Karel Roessingh, a modernist "on the right." In 1915, he stated that the heyday of positivism fortunately had passed and that now "our eyes

---

34. So Bowler 1990, 207.
35. Initially, Edward Aveling (1851–1898) lived with (the later theosophist) Annie Besant and from 1884 with the daughter of Karl Marx, the tragic Eleanor (1855–1898).
36. Dutch positivistic theologians were Opzoomer, the later J. H. Scholten, Kuenen, and Tiele (cf. Bril 1986, 251f.; Jongeneel 1971).
37. Van den Berg 1984, 206–7, 214, 216, 218.

desire to look especially at Germany's spiritual heroes from yesteryear"—neo-Idealism indeed.[38] Theologians "cannot neglect to raise the question as to where reason is, the εἶδος, *die Vernunft*... and then there is only one place to start: to enter our own mind seek out that which is greater than our own mind." One cannot make it, according to Roessingh, without "reason as such" (G. *die Vernunft überhaupt*), the "descendant" of Plato's realm of ideas (232). Roessingh sees a historical relationship with Plato's ideas, but also a new phase in the course of this development. "We know nothing that goes beyond our experience, but there is a way of considering things for which you need Reason" (G. *eine Vernunftnotwendige Betrachtungsweise*).

Today, people talk about "instrumental reason." This is exactly the same notion as Vollenhoven's "reason as method."[39]

C. A GLANCE BACK AT THE ROUTE TRAVELED THUS FAR

We now interrupt our study to look back and raise anew the question as to what precisely time-currents and types are. Every type concerns an interpretation of the created cosmos and, in that sense, of interpreted facts—the relationship between matter, life, and the soul; whether nature and humans are determined or free; and how humans and animals are related. In short, a type pertains to ontology, the study of being.

A time-current pertains to the foundation of human knowledge (a priori or not), to what in a general sense is considered normative, as well as the question of good and evil, and to the criteria for sound science. Within a certain time-current, one type or a complex of types can be dominant. For instance, in the Middle Ages, Scholasticism dominated; in the Renaissance, the occult tradition (hermetic Kabbalism) prevailed. But if the descriptions above are true, then we cannot say that a certain time-current belongs only to the type that dominates in that period.[40]

Briefly put: Types are related to the question how humans and the world are put together or structured, that is, to ontology, while time-currents pertain to the question concerning the foundation of human knowledge and normativity.[41]

---

38. Although Vollenhoven nowhere mentioned Roessingh, his neo-Idealism is evident to any who examine his works.
39. Members of the Frankfurter school used the term *instrumental reason*. We will use it here as synonymous with Vollenhoven's phrase *reason as method*.
40. For the distinction between types and time-currents, the reader is reminded of Centore's reference to "cross-divisions" (cf. p. 62 above).
41. As for the relationship between Vollenhoven's problem-historical method and his own systematic philosophy, see Bril 1986, 188–91; and Tol 1993. Vollenhoven's method does

As we continue our review of the course of the history of philosophy, we will want to ask ourselves whether this thesis holds true for the twentieth century as well.

V. Irrationalism and the Struggle for Truth

The era of late Rationalism is succeeded by a fundamental shift in Western thought (c. 1900), namely, by the rise of philosophical Irrationalism.

Vollenhoven distinguished three overlapping periods: pragmatism, the philosophy of life, and existentialism, respectively.[42] (The overlapping is not unusual.) This does not reflect a sequence in origin but rather in dominance. Pragmatism was for years the leading philosophy in America, while existentialism was in vogue in western Europe after World War II. The philosophy of life drew large crowds between the two world wars, notably in the intellectual life of Germany during the Weimar Republic (1919–1933).

Among the early representatives associated with this turnabout at the close of the nineteenth century, Vollenhoven mentioned the following persons (with the year of their birth):

- pragmatism: William James (1842), John Dewey (1859), and Sigmund Freud (1856);
- the philosophy of life: Friedrich Nietzsche (1844), Henri Bergson (1959), Max Weber (1864), and Ernst Troeltsch (1865); and
- existentialism: Søren Kierkegaard (1813).[43]

Meanwhile, other philosophical developments occurred. One could add currents of thought such as structuralism, neo-Marxism, New Age, and postmodernism. Treating each of these movements separately is not as much our concern as is the question of Vollenhoven's interpretation of the character and the problem of twentieth-century time-currents.

Let us first listen to Irrationalism and, after that, to the bitter struggle for truth.

---

not follow straightaway from his systematic philosophy. It is the result of trial and error over the years (Bril 1986, 181–83). Four other methodologies preceded his problem-historical method (which he unfolded at age fifty two).

42. In later years, Vollenhoven (1965a, 111) distinguished four periods within Irrationalism: neopositivism, pragmatism, philosophy of life, and existentialism. His student Henk Hart drew the distinction between pragmatism and neopositivism (1966, 7).

43. Vollenhoven 1956b, 40–42; 1962d, 1964c.

A. IRRATIONALISM

During the era of Rationalism, autonomous human beings maintained their certainty in a high-handed, autonomous reason. With the arrival of the new Irrationalism, reason's reach was restricted. Fixed norms and indubitable certainties vanished. Humans beings were faced with a crisis that Nietzsche foresaw and described in one of his last works, *Ecce Homo:*

> One day my name will be associated with the memory of something tremendous—a crisis without equal on earth, the most profound collision of conscience, a decision that was conjured up *against* everything that had been believed, demanded, hallowed so far. (1967, 326)

Years later, John Dewey spoke of a similar crisis ". . . in which man is now involved all over the world, in all aspects of his life. . . ."[44]

Van den Berg viewed the time around 1900 as the beginning of a new metabletic period, as a "spiritual revolution," which he treated extensively in his *Gedane Zaken.* He cited an interesting piece from the French writer André Gide from 1899 (1977, 48f.). The story is about the "gratuitous act" of a person who for no reason at all mutilates the face of another person. Van den Berg noted: "There is no public morality, no generally recognized sense of decency. Everyone determines for himself what is good or not good, admissible or inadmissible." He then asked the pertinent question: ". . . according to what should goodness and badness, admissibility and inadmissibility possibly be measured, when the standard of a generally accepted, majority-shared norm is lacking?" (51).

Let us next listen to Friedrich Nietzsche, whose publications preceded those of Gide. In the first part of his *Thus Spoke Zarathustra,* that is, at the beginning of Nietzsche's third main period, he took distance from all tradition (Fretz 1980, 108f.), introducing an Irrationalistic period, which many designated as the philosophy of life.[45] For three hundred years, the reason of autonomous mankind had reigned supreme. Nietzsche, however, dared to doubt, even deny, this rational knowledge: "trust reason—why not mistrust it?" (*Werke* iii, 517). We draw unjust conclusions, according to Nietzsche, when we place "blind trust in reason" (ibid, 883). As he saw it, "the a priori elements of knowledge are useful mistakes" (*HWP* i, 471).

---

44. Dewey 1957, xxi. Cf. Hart 1966, 4, 10–12.
45. *Lebensphilosophie.* Rickert 1920; Baumgartner 1969; and Vollenhoven 1964a, 197–200, and "Nietzsche" *OE.*

Vollenhoven summarized several issues thus:

> The a priori concepts of the understanding were cast aside, and with that reason was dethroned. The ideal now is to go beyond good and evil, to replace these with the opposition between what is and is not outstanding. (1964a, 199)

A "transvaluation of all values" is necessary. Nietzsche was convinced that "revering truth is the result of an illusion" (*Werke* iii, 424), for "there is no truth at all . . . every consideration of truth is necessarily false" or "the most extreme form of nihilism" (ibid, 555; *HWP* vi, 850). That is how Nietzsche viewed himself as Europe's "first complete nihilist," who, all the same, had already left nihilism behind. He sought a complete break with the traditional values of reason and morality (Ries 1977, 77–88). For him, nihilism meant "that the highest values have been transvalued" (*Werke* iii, 140).

It is interesting to compare Vollenhoven's historical approach to Nietzsche with that of Reinier Beerling, a philosopher at the University of Leiden, the more so because there is no spiritual kinship between Beerling, the atheist (1979, 9: "I consider myself a committed and simultaneously obstinate but tolerant atheist"), and Vollenhoven, the Christian.

Beerling approached Nietzsche's stance from the perspective of the history of reason. "Nietzsche . . . stands at the end of the line of development within European thought that commences with the discovery of rational human subjectivity as the most profound and indubitable foundation for an objective worldview" (1977, 40). This development started with Descartes: "Deep within himself man discovered reason as the new *absolute given*" and ended with a spiritual catastrophe for Nietzsche (41). "Humankind, thinking mankind, having founded its autonomy on reason, once again becomes heteronomous, this time not vis-à-vis God, but vis-à-vis the irrational claims of *life*." Beerling concluded, "In the nineteenth century, Nietzsche is the highest expression of a rationalistically founded European subjectivity turning into nihilism" (46).

Banning characterized Nietzsche's point of view with words from his *The Antichrist*:

> What is good? Everything that heightens the feeling of power in man, the will to power, power itself.
> What is bad? Everything that is born of weakness.[46]

---

46. Banning 1965, 64. Nietzsche 1954, (§2) 570.

Johan de Graaf summarized Nietzsche's view thus: ". . . goodness is good only . . . when it sprouts forth from the arbitrariness of the strong individual, who could have acted differently" (1961, 23). Strong persons create their own values. In this way, a passive nihilism becomes an active nihilism.

For people like the German philologist Nietzsche and the Spanish philosopher Ortega y Gasset,[47] the aristocratic elite still possessed the creative ability to determine what counted as good and evil. This ability was subsequently democratized: "Authenticity has replaced morality as the standard for human adequacy. . . . [with authenticity defined as:] do it if it makes you feel good" (Phillips 1985, 171).

This development has been summarized as follows:

> During the last two centuries nihilism . . . appears to have landed in a new phase. Better put: Western thought in its entirety has entered its nihilistic phase. Nihilism is no longer peculiar, heretical, it is no longer nourished by doubts regarding the highest value, but by a certainty regarding the lack of values.[48]

One can describe a historical development as well as evaluate it. Vollenhoven would do that, I think, as follows. When Nietzsche stated that human reason and a priori knowledge of laws are figments of the imagination, Vollenhoven would concur. When Nietzsche then stated that nothing is intrinsically normative, that there are absolutely no laws to which humans must subject themselves, Vollenhoven would be diametrically opposed to Nietzsche. As he wrote, "The opposition good – evil is replaced with high – low. Nietzsche wants nothing to do with a law that holds for the cosmos, according to which we must test our deeds: the reality in which we now live is the only one" ("Nietzsche" *OE*).

Are there definite norms for good and evil? In the eighth century B.C., Amos, a shepherd and a dresser of sycamore trees from Tekoa, prophesized: "But let justice roll down like waters, and righteousness like an ever-flowing stream" (Amos 5:24). André Gide did not believe that prophetic picture, claiming as he did that there is no knowledge of justice within mankind, and that there are no laws outside of mankind. He was influenced in this regard by Nietzsche, whose words we cited earlier:

> One day my name will be associated with the memory of something tremendous—a crisis without equal on earth, the most profound collision of conscience, a decision that was conjured up *against* everything that had been believed, demanded, hallowed so far. (1967, 326)

---

47. Cf. Zijlstra 1982, 1, 6, 9, 181, and 188.
48. *Filosofie en Practijk* 5, 1984, 111.

B. DECISIONISM: MAX WEBER AND ALBERT EINSTEIN

The history of a priori ideas, norms, and values does not always end in a denial of all norms. We now see another conviction emerge.

Max Weber (1864–1920), a famous economist and sociologist, in contrast to Nietzsche, appreciated the Rational method. Science, such as the discipline of economics, can promote and direct, if not realize, much. As a science, however, economics cannot insure the direction of its goals. That is a personal choice or a political decision—hence Habermas's characterization *decisionism*. Reason remains but limits itself to an analysis of ways of realizing a supra-Rational ideal. Some spoke, judgmentally, of "reason halved": the Rational method pertains only to science as method; goals and objectives are supra-Rational decisions.[49]

The neo-Kantians resisted Weber's view, initiating a "struggle regarding values" (G. *Werturteitstreit*), later designated as the second struggle concerning method.[50]

A similar kind of decisionism is found in the writings of Albert Einstein.[51] The originator of the theory of relativity wrote: "For science can only ascertain what *is*, but not what *should be*, and outside of its domain value judgments of all kinds remain necessary. Religion . . . deals only with evaluations of human thought and action" (1954, 45). Religion must establish goals and objectives; science can teach us a few things about the means by which these objectives can be reached: "Science without religion is lame, religion without science is blind" (ibid., 46). Einstein's way of stating it conveys for many an impressive and sympathetic standpoint. And yet, it contains a horrible snare.

Besides Weber and Einstein, the Nobel Prize–winner Peter Medawar[52] and the philosopher Karl Popper maintained the doctrine of so-called half reason, namely, that the use of reason pertains to means, while supra-Rational decisions determine objectives.

The German jurist Carl Schmitt (1888–1985), already an authority in the years before the rise of National Socialism, proclaimed that the ulti-

---

49. Concerning Weber's decisionism, see Turner and Factor 1984; for the relationship between ethics and science according to Weber, see De Valk 1971, 148–51.
50. The proclaimed bifurcation between the two aspects is debatable from the viewpoint of theoretical science (cf. Griffioen 1990, 57f.).
51. Vollenhoven reckoned Einstein, as well as Weber, to belong to those thinkers espousing the philosophy of life viewpoint. He also pointed to a typological connection between Spinoza and Einstein, namely, a limited parallelism (cf. pp. 59 and 63 above; also his 1956b, 34, 41 ["parallelism without atomism"]). See further Bril 1986, 141–42.
52. See Bril 1986, 347.

mate source of justice was an act of decision.[53] Decisionism, according to Schmitt, concerns "an absolute decision that is neither reasoned nor debated, needs not justify itself, and hence is created out of nothing."[54] "Viewed normatively, this decision is born out of nothing" (1934, according to *HWP* ii, 160f.).[55]

H. H. Dietze, a German jurist who applied this thesis to the relationship between the Jews and the German Aryans, wrote in 1936: "Justice is that which Aryans consider justice, injustice is that which they throw away."[56] That was a subjective decision, which those who survived the massacre looked back on with stunned horror.

It is no wonder that others talked about a crisis in Western philosophy, as did Herman Dooyeweerd, who in his book *The Crisis of the Humanistic Doctrine of the State* called Schmitt's view "irrationalistic decisionism" (1931, 70).

When Jürgen Habermas looked back at the war years (1940–1945), he spoke with horror about decisionism and half reason in his "Struggle Concerning Positivism."[57] Good and evil as well as righteousness cannot and may not be a purely subjective decision, according to him. Rejecting half reason in favor of a broader view of reason, he likewise wished to arrive at a rational solution for objectives, too, in terms of communicative rationality. Habermas's opponent, Hans Albert, one of Popper's close associates, considered, in turn, communicative rationality an impossibility and "total reason" to be a myth.

The main issue appears to be again the place and status of reason. Kant, in his *Critique of Pure Reason*, put it in the form of three questions: What can I know? What ought I to do? and What may I hope for? In

---

53. Helmut Kuhn 1967, 314. In 1921, Schmitt introduced the positive term *decisionism* (*HWP* ii, 160–61), that is, after Weber's death. Habermas picked up the term but used it in a negative sense (*HWP* iv, 587).
54. This professor of constitutional and international law in Berlin became a member of National Socialism and supplied a theoretical foundation for German constitutional law. Schmitt also spoke of a "necessary conflict with the Jewish mind": "I repeat forever and ever the urgent plea to read every sentence in Adolf Hitler's *Mein Kampf* about the Jewish question" (Staff 1964, 172). We should keep this in mind when reading the sentence "Viewed normatively, this decision is born out of nothing."
55. Karl Löwith referred to the kinship between Schmitt and Weber regarding their division between facts and norms (1940, 166–76); he also combated, as early as 1935, "political decisionism" (see Bril 1986, 347).
56. According to Hommes 1961, 82.
57. The discussion stemming from the first phase of the third struggle concerning method can be found in a collection of articles written by both parties and put together by Adorno (1974); cf. Bril 1986, 267–71.

brief, it concerns the legitimate use of reason in terms of its scope and its possibilities.

Contemporary postmodernism follows the path set by Nietzsche. There are remarkable parallels between the debate about positivism and about postmodernism, which took off in 1980 and initially engaged Habermas and Jean-François Lyotard, a French postmodernist.[58]

C. VOLLENHOVEN'S VIEW OF TIME-CURRENTS: A FIRST BALANCE

At the beginning of this chapter, we noted that a controversy about the criteria for a good scientific method continues. The conflict regarding positivism and the debate within postmodernism are proof of this fact. As cited earlier, according to historian of science Laudan, *"These norms . . . have been perhaps the single major source for most of the controversies in the history of science."* Though not identical, his thesis is certainly compatible with Vollenhoven's characterization of time-currents as relating to changing views of what grounds normativity.

Plato looked for transcendent normative standards that held for all. Centuries later, philosophers considered these standards to be within the human mind a priori. On November 10, 1793, the French publicly honored the "goddess of reason" in Paris's Notre Dame Cathedral (Praamsma iii, 9). Within one hundred years—for some, anyway—norms had become merely a personal and usually contingent creation. And the struggle continues—concerning the place and the truth of divine order and of human systems (G. *Ordnungen*): "The conflict concerning the truth of *Ordnungen* is the real substance of history" (*HWP* vi, 1298).

There is clearly a remarkable concurrence between what the *Historisches Wörterbuch* highlighted as "the real substance of history" and Laudan suggested is *"perhaps the single major source for most of the controversies in the history of science"* and Vollenhoven's characterization of time-currents as relating to changing views of what grounds normativity. But while other authors may advance similar interpretations of different parts of this historic process, Vollenhoven was possibly the only one who tried to trace this theme consistently—from the ancient Greeks to his own century. Our exploratory journey has only confirmed the sense of his project.

---

58. For agreements and disagreements between the views of Vollenhoven and those of the postmodernists, see Tol 1992.

VI. Synthesis, Secularization, and Time-Currents

Is there not more to say about the real substance of history? A deeper dimension? Adriaan Peperzak, for example, observed that "even if it is perhaps unreachable, truth does not cease to control all philosophy" (1992, 156). What is truth? Christ said to his disciples: "I am the way, and the truth, and the life" (John 14:6).[59] Are there no links here? In this connection, we refer to the history of secularization, in the sense of secularism or unbelief.[60]

A. SYNTHESIS AND THE THREE MAIN PERIODS

Vollenhoven believed that a good deal of the history of philosophy is dominated by synthesis: namely, by an attempted assimilation of Christian faith and Greco-Roman thought that ties together "pagan conceptions and themes of the Word revelation" ("Synthesis" *OE*). This question is so important to him that he arranged the entire history of philosophy around the issue of synthesis.

> In the patristic period (A.D. 50–c. 650), the synthesis had an original character to it. Already then, the two worlds of thought were connected in a variety of ways. Most thinkers raised in a Christian milieu went about their work biblicisticly: they unconsciously read their former pagan concepts into the Scriptures, only to retrieve these again, now clothed with divine authority, from the Word revelation. ("Wijsbegeerte" *OE*)

On this basis, Vollenhoven came to divide the history of philosophy into three main periods: (1) the period before the synthesis, (2) the time of the synthesis, espoused by the church fathers and then by the medieval Scholastics, and (3) "modern philosophy" (after c. 1450). The last main period,

> . . . certainly among its leading movements, is characterized by a strong anti-synthetic trait. The synthesis prominently highlighted during the preceding period was rejected; although the reasons given were clearly different. Most thinkers distanced themselves from the Christian dimension in synthesis philosophy, others rejected its specifically pagan elements. ("Wijsbegeerte" *OE*)

---

59. Translator's note: In his *Commentary on the Gospel of John*, John Calvin wrote, "If any man turns aside from Christ he can do nothing but go astray. If any man does not rest on Him, he will feed elsewhere on nothing but wind and vanity. If any aims beyond Him, he will find death instead of life" (2, 77).
60. The distinction between secularization and secularism has gained in familiarity; see Gogarten 1953 and Nijk 1968, 52–59.

This divergence manifested itself with the Renaissance and the Reformation. Non-Christian thinking became more and more influential in philosophy as the synthesis waned.[61]

B. RELIGION AND ITS TIES WITH TYPES AND TIME-CURRENTS

This basic religious stance has to do with the position one chooses with respect to the complex of types as well as to time-currents.

Types

As mentioned at the end of Part Three, Vollenhoven was convinced that few types comport well with the biblical message (even when fused in a constructed synthesis). Combining the Christian faith with the consistent dualism of the Manicheans or with a consistent monism and the doctrine of emanation makes for an odd fit at most. The same incompatibility thesis applies to the doctrine of reincarnation held to by the Pythagoreans and Plato as well as to the Averroïstic notion of a world soul.[62]

One's worldview—one's faith—exerts an influence on the way one looks at humanity. For instance, in Darwin's day, the question was debated whether humans were created in the image of God, that is, whether they were stewards of God's creation[63] or whether they were really only mammals, a view critically typified by Van den Berg as "animalism" (1984, 120, 186).

Time-Currents

In addition to its relation to typology, this basic religious attitude also pertains to one's view of reason and the position one chooses regarding time-currents. In contrast to Foucault's argument, humans need not be

---

61. Vollenhoven 1932b, 70 (Dutch *de tijd der wijkende synthese*). Herman Dooyeweerd, like his brother-in-law Vollenhoven, used the term *synthesis* to mean a synthesis of pagan and Christian motifs (1953, 189, 520; 1958, 236; 1979, Chapter 5), but he often preferred the term *accommodation* (cf. 1958, 2).

62. The notion of mono-psychism, according to Vollenhoven, is typologically related to later psycho-monism (Bril 1986, 321).

63. According to Groen van Prinsterer, the image of God in humanity signifies that humans are clothed with power and, as God's servants and stewards, are called to utilize "each in his own circle," their entrusted talents "to the advantage of others" (Van Dijk 1989, 106). Cf. Groen, *Ongeloof en Revolutie* 1886, 48; *Bescheiden* II 1991, 126.
   There is a remarkable kinship between Groen's view of the basic philosophical lines and the views of Dooyeweerd and Vollenhoven (cf. Zwaan 1972). See further Van der Walt 1978, 120–30; Kamphuis 1986; Noordegraaf 1990; and Van Genderen and Velema 1992, 292–353.

exponents of *epistemes* or of the *Zeitgeist*. Friedrich Jacobi made a clear distinction between his view and that of Immanuel Kant, who favored autonomous reason, a view Jacobi labeled "self-divination."

Let us take a closer look at the time-currents in the three main periods.

Vollenhoven's division is not customarily used as an interpretation of the history of philosophy. It is a surprise, then, to learn that a convinced atheist like Beerling wrote that "the supreme mark of the entire post-medieval culture [is] secularization" and that the historian Peter Gay characterized the Enlightenment as "the rise of modern paganism" (1967).

Rationalists, wishing to be independent and autonomous, used reason to devise their own picture of God and guidelines for ethics. Possessing the inner light of reason, they did not say, "Thy word is a lamp to my feet and a light to my path" (Psalm 119:105). They may have conceded that Scripture can contain truths, but to them reason was the real criterion; humans would find the supra-arbitrary norms (the law) in themselves. This a priorizing, i.e., transferring the universal law from outside of the mind to inside of the mind (1956b, 19), grew rapidly in the sixteenth century. But why not earlier, let us say in the period of the synthesis? Henk Hart correctly observed, "During this period the doctrine of reason could not come to full development because of the power of divine authority" (1966, 3).

Possessing reason as they did, humans were autonomous, that is to say, a law unto themselves. Fichte embraced "an uninterrupted making of the law by a rational being for itself" (G. *eine ununterbrochene Gesetzgebung des vernünftigen Wesens an sich selbst, HWP* i, 709) and rejected God's revelation as revelation, viewing it only as heteronomous, improper coercion from the outside.

C. TURNOVER OF TIME-CURRENTS

The history of time-currents is a process of continual changes, with ever-new tensions and conflicts. What is the cause of all this? As I see it, there are two main causes: confrontation with reality and the process of secularization.

Confrontation with Reality

When current theory confronts the evidence of empirical reality, an unavoidable revision may result. A few examples may serve to illustrate this point.

On the basis of reason, Descartes concluded that light did not need time to travel. But "should experience show that light needs time to travel, then my entire philosophy would collapse" (quoted on p. 81 above). In this way, he could also deduce the laws of collision. Both deductions appeared later not to correspond with experience.

Rousseau judged that the state of nature had to be constructed by means of reason, aided therein by imagination.

In his embryological theory of encapsulation, Bonnet interpreted ever-smaller egg cells as little boxes in still smaller boxes as a triumph of pure reason. And Schelling claimed that "the natural sciences unfold everything a priori" (G. *die Naturwissenschaften entfalten alles a priori*).

From humans' moral sense, Shaftesbury could deduce a naturally given innate ability, a universal ethics, which the positivist Littré in turn could not accept. Reason, it seems, though revered deeply, continually appeared to make mistakes.

The positivists did display an adamant intellectual asceticism—but that was a necessary reaction to the intellectual boastfulness of early Rationalism. With good reason, they saw "reality as an arbiter."[64]

Those striving to arrive at a philosophy in the light of Scripture can reap a certain advantage from the results of such discussions between time-currents. But we can go a step further, walking in the steps of C. Vonk and Jacob Klapwijk. Vonk spoke, on behalf of ancient Israel, of the "great annexation," namely, of several issues from the surrounding cultures, which in the process received another meaning (1960, 493–96). Klapwijk points more than once in his publications to the need for transformation.[65] For him, it was more than merely a matter of "moments of truth" held by non-Christian thinkers.[66]

The Process of Secularization

One catalyst for the change in time-currents seems to have to do with the interplay of current theory and experienced reality. But given Hart's suggestion that the doctrine of reason could not fully develop during the time of the synthesis "because of the power of divine author-

---

64. Duijker 1980, 70–74 (cf. 51, 66, 79).
65. In contrast to Jacob Klapwijk and in agreement with I. Bernhard Cohen (1985, 631) and his close associate Everett Mendelsohn (1985), we use the term "transformation" for the *Umdeuting* ("reinterpretation") of a type in the following time-current.
66. Klapwijk (1987), along with a critical commentary by A. P. Bos, ibid., 135–38.

ity," might there also be a connection between the process of secularization and the changes in time-currents?

In the third main period, the time of antisynthetic thinking (or the aversion to synthesis), secularization did increase continually, as Rudolf Boon pointed out in his thorough "investigation into the rise of West-European atheism" (1976). The process of secularization also constituted an important precondition for the development of evolutionism within positivism. Charles Darwin waited twenty years before publishing his ideas concerning evolution and evolutionism, keeping his hunches to himself for quite some time. According to Ruse, once *The Origin of Species* (1859) was published, he was able to secure room for his animalistic view of humanity because modernism was on the increase among the general population and amid the theologians—evident, for example, in the collection of *Essays and Reviews* (1860).[67] Ruse also referred to Matthew Arnold, a literary man, who, preferring Hellenism to "Hebraism," "wrote on religion as being only ethics heightened, enkindled, lit up by feeling" (1979, 242). The agnostic Darwin was buried in Westminster Abbey in 1872, accompanied by an impressive ecclesiastical ceremony. The *Zeitgeist*—the spirit of the age—certainly had changed (Bril 1993).

Friedrich Nietzsche believed that humans were saved by secularization (*Werke* ii, 978). In his own words, "We deny God, we deny our responsibility before God, thereby we save first of all the world." "We save?" Jean-Paul Sartre, the French existentialist, cynically, said it a bit differently: "The existentialist . . . finds it extremely embarrassing that God does not exist, for there disappears with Him all possibility of finding values in an intelligible heaven. There can no longer be any good *à priori*" (1956, 294). Sartre continued, "Dostoevsky once wrote 'If God did not exist, everything would be permitted'; and that, for existentialism, is the starting point. Everything is indeed permitted if God does not exist" (ibid., 294–95).

After World War II, Max Horkheimer and Theodor Adorno, Jewish thinkers from Germany, observed that our culture still refuses to acknowledge "the impossibility of deriving from reason any fundamental argument against murder" (1972, 118). Michel Foucault claimed straight out, "For modern thought, no morality is possible" (1970, 328). The receding synthesis, increasing unbelief, constitutes a great power in the struggle during successive historical periods. We are reminded of the

---

67. Ruse 1979, 240; cf. Kamphuis 1986, 51.

verdict that the "conflict concerning the truth of ordinances is the real substance of history."

The twentieth-century folk singer Bob Dylan voiced the complaint of countless young people: "I have nothing, ma, to live up to."[68]

Death and Life

At times, an unexpectedly wonderful revival can be had.[69] In Russia, even before the political comeback in 1989, in spite of decades-long terrorism against the Christian faith,[70] a new movement was formed by young people who again began to look for faith and who gained a new appreciation for God's valid norms. The historian M. C. Smit made that point on more than one occasion. In his terms, he spoke of the "first history" breaking through into the "second history," sometimes entirely unexpectedly.[71]

There is renewed hope, as the Psalmist expresses God's care for his creation thus: "and thou renewest the face of the earth" (Psalm 104:30 KJV) and the prophet sees that "the desert shall rejoice, and blossom as the rose" (Isaiah 35:1 KJV).

---

68. Cf. Zijlstra 1982, 188. [Translator's note: Dylan's popular song, "Blowin' in the Wind" (1962) is a bit more positive: The answers to several important human questions can be obtained, as they are blowing in the wind.]
69. See also what is called "het Reveil" in the nineteenth century and the Reformation in the sixteenth century.
70. See Buss 1987 and Van der Bercken 1989.
71. Smit 2002, 363–379. The first history (the transcendental meaning of historical events) "can be acknowledged, followed and obeyed, but it can also be ignored, transgressed, violated and fiercely combated. In other words, this original history is of a *normative* character" (370–371). Arie van Dijk, a student of Smit, expressly joined Groen van Prinsterer when he wrote, "In summary, Groen's view boils down to this: Whereas the historical effect of the notion of revolution derived its irresistible driving power from an immobile conviction, it met simultaneously its superior opponent in the unchanging creation ordinances" (1991, 104).

WORKS CITED

Adorno, Theodor W. *Der Positivismusstreit in der deutschen Soziologie.* 3rd ed. Darmstadt: Luchterhand, 1974.

Agassi, Joseph. "Continuity and the history of science." *Jouranl of the History of Ideas* 34 (1973): 609–626.

———. *Science in Flux.* Dordrecht: Reidel, 1975.

Baarda, Tjitze, ed., *Het Evangelie van Thomas.* Zoetermeer: Meinema, 1999.

———. "The Gospel of Thomas and the Old Testament." *Proceedings of the Irish Biblical Association.* No. 26 (2003): 1–28.

———. "The Gospel of Thomas." *Proceedings of the Irish Biblical Association.* No. 26 (2003): 46–65.

Bakker, Reinout. *Het anonieme denken: Michel Foucault en het structuralisme.* Baarn: Wereldvenster, 1973.

Banning, Willem. *Typen van zedenleer.* 3rd ed. Haarlem: Bohn, 1965.

Baumgartner, H. M. "Lebensphilosophie." In Vol. 1, *Bilanz der Theologie im 20. Jahrhundert,* 290–296. Freiburg: Herder, 1969.

Beerling, Reinier Franciscus. *Niet te geloven: wijsgerig schaatsen op godgeleerd ijs.* Deventer: Van Loghum Slaterus, 1979.

———. *Van Nietzsche tot Heidegger.* Deventer: Van Loghum Slaterus, 1977.

Begemann, A. W. *Aanvangen der griekse wijsbegeerte.* Groningen: Vuurbaak, 1975.

Berger, H. H. "Idee." In *Woordenboek Filosofie.* Edited by W. H. M. Willemsen. Assen: Van Gorcum (1992): 206.

Berkouwer, Gerrit C. *The Person of Christ.* Grand Rapids: Eerdmans, 1954. (2nd ed., 1963; 3rd ed., 1968; 4th ed., 1980). Original ed.: *De Persoon van Christus.* Kampen: Kok, 1952.

———. *General Revelation.* Grand Rapids: Eerdmans, 1955. Original ed.: *De algemene openbaring.* Kampen: Kok, 1951.

———. *The Church.* Grand Rapids: Eerdmans, 1976. Original ed.: *De kerk II.* Kampen: Kok, 1972.

Boendermaker, J. P. *Luther: Brieven uit de beslissende jaren van zijn leven.* Baarn: Ten Have, 1982.

Boon, Rudolf. *Het christendom op de tocht: Een onderzoek naar de opkomst van het westerse atheïsme.* Kampen: Kok, 1976.

Bos, Abraham P. "Het grondmotief van de Griekse cultuur en het Titanisch zin-perspectief." *Philosophia Reformata* 51 (1986): 117–37.

———. (1991a) *In de greep van de Titanen: Een inleiding tot een hoofdstroming van de Griekse filosofie.* Amsterdam: Buijten & Schipperheijn, 1991.

99

————. (1991b) "Van nachtuilskuiken tot arendsoog: Aristoteles over de conditie van de mens." In *Grote filosofen*. Edited by J. Davidse. Kampen: Kok (1991): 39–62.

Bos, D. J. *Michel Foucault in gesprek*. Amsterdam, 1985.

Bowler, Peter J. *The Non-Darwinian Revolution: Reinterpreting a Historical Myth*. Baltimore: John Hopkins, 1988.

————. *Charles Darwin*. Oxford: Basil Blackwell, 1990.

Brandt, Hartmut. *Untersuchungen zur Lehre von den angeborenen Ideen*. Meissenheim am Glan: Hain, 1977.

Breman, Christine M. *The Association of Evangelicals in Africa*. Zoetermeer: Boekencentrum, 1998.

Bril, Kornelis A. *Tien jaar probleemhistorische methode. Bibliografie en overzichten over de jaren* 1960–1970. Amsterdam: Vrije Universiteit, 1971.

————. "A Selected and Annotated Bibliography of D. H. Th. Vollenhoven." *Philosophia Reformata* 38 (1973): 212–28.

————. *Vollenhoven's laatste werk 1970–1975*. Amsterdam: VU Boekhandel, 1982.

————. *Westerse denkstructuren*. PhD. Diss. Amsterdam: Vrije Universiteit, 1986.

————. See: Tol and Bril.

————. "De opkomst en de ontwikkeling van het evolutionisme en de probleemhistorische methode van Vollenhoven." *Philosophia Reformata* 58 (1993): 28–48.

————. "A Comparison between Dooyeweerd and Vollenhoven on the Historiography of Philosophy." *Philosophia Reformata* 60 (1995): 121–46.

————. "Lexicon en redactioneel commentaar." In *Schematisch Kaarten. Filosofische Concepties in Probleemhistorisch verband*. By D. H. Th. Vollenhoven. Edited by K. A. Bril and P. J. Boonstra. Amstelveen: De Zaak Haes, 2000.

————. "Publications to appear on the Problem-Historical Method: An overview of work in progress." *Vollenhoven Newsletter* No. 1 July 2003: 2–4. Email journal.

Broad, C. D. *The Mind and Its Place in Nature*. London: Routledge, 1925.

Buber, Martin. *I and Thou*. Translated by W. Kaufmann. New York: Scribner, 1970.

Burtt, Edwin Arnold. *The Metaphysical Foundations of Modern Physical Science*. London: Routledge, 1924 (rev. ed. 1932).

Buss, G. *The Bear's Hug: Religious Belief in the Soviet State,* Hodder and Stoughton 1987.

Bynum, W. F., ed. *Dictionary of the History of Science*. London: Macmillan, 1981.

Calvin, John. *Institutes of the Christian Religion*. Edited by J.T. McNeill. Translated by F. L. Battles. Philadelphia: Westminster, 1960.

————.*Commentary of the Gospel of John,* Torrance edition. (Grand Rapids: Eerdmans, 1994.

Capek, Milic. "Change." *Encylopedia of Philosophy*. 2 (1967): 75–79.

Centore, F. F. *Persons:* A *comparative Account of the Six Possible Theories*. Westport, CN: Greenwood, 1979.

Choi, Yong Joon. *Dialog and Antithesis. A Philosophical Study on the Significance of Herman Dooyeweerd's Transcendental Critique*. PhD diss. Potchefstroomse Universiteit, 2000.

Christelijke encyclopaedie. Edited by F. W. Grosheide and G. P. van Itterson. 6 vols. 2nd ed. Kampen: Kok, 1956–1961.

Cobb, John. *A Christian Natural Theology: Based on the Thought of Alfred North White-head*. Philadelphia: Westminster, 1965.

Cohen, I. Bernard. *Revolution in Science*. Cambridge, MA: Harvard University Press, 1985.

Da Costa, Isaäc. *Bezwaren tegen de Geest der Eeuw*. Translated by K. Exalto. Blieswijk: Tolle Lege, 1974. (1st ed. 1823).

Darwin, Charles. *The Life and Letters of Charles Darwin*. Edited by Francis Darwin. London: J. Murray, 1887.

De Boer, Theodorus. *De ontwikkelingsgang in het denken van Husserl*. Assen: Van Gorcum, 1966.

————. *De God van de filosofen en de God van Pascal: Op het gransgebied van filosofie en theologie*. 's-Gravenhage: Meinema, 1989.

De Fontenay, E. *Diderot: ou le matérialisme enchanté*. Paris: Grasset, 1981.

De Graaf, Johannes. *De ethiek van het immoralisme*. Nijkerk: Callenbach, 1961.

De Rijk, L. M. *Middeleeuwse wijsbegeerte*. Assen: Van Gorcum, 1977.

De Strycker, E. *Beknopte geschiedenis van de antieke filosofie*. 2nd ed. Antwerp: Neder-landsche Boekhandel, 1980 (1st ed. 1967).

De Valk, J. M. M. "Max Weber," in *Geschiedenis van de sociologie*. H. P. M. Goddijn et al. Meppel: Boom, 1971, 145–63.

De Vogel, Cornelia J. "De continuïteit van het West-Europese denken." *ANTWP* 42 (1950): 177–90.

————. "Averroës als verklaarder van Aristoteles en zijn invloed op het West-Europese denken." *ANTWP* 50 (1958): 225–40.

————. *Theoria: studies over de griekse wisjbegeerte*. Assen: Van Gorcum, 1967.

————. *De grondslag van onze zekerheid*. Assen: Van Gorcum, 1977.

De Vries, Gerrit Jacob. *Inleiding tot het denken van Plato*. 3rd ed. Amsterdam, 1957. (4th ed. 1966).

De Wolff, I. *De strijd om de kerk in de 19e eeuw 1815–1834*. Enschede: Boersma, 1954.

Delfgaauw, B. M. I. *Beknopte geschiedenis der wijsbegeerte*. 3 vols. Amsterdam: Wereld-venster, 1950–1952,

————. "Terug naar de werkelijkheid." *Wijsgerig Perspectief* 4 (1988/89): 126–28.

Descartes, R. *The Philosophical Works of Descartes*. Translated by Elizabeth S. Haldane and G. R. T. Ross. 2 vols. Cambridge: Cambridge University Press, 1911.

Desmond, Adrian U. J., and James R. Moore. *Darwin*. London: Michel Joseph, 1991.

Dewey, John. *Reconstruction in Philosophy*. Boston: Beacon, 1957.

Dictionary of the History of Ideas. 5 vols. Edited by Philip Wiener. New York: Scrib-ner's, 1968.

Diderot, Denis. *Lettres à Sophie Volland*. 2 vols. Paris: Gallimard, 1950.

————. *Le rêve de d'Alembert* (1769). in *Œvres philosophiques*. Edited by P. Vernière. Paris (1956): 285–371.

Diederich, Werner. *Theorie–Diskussion. Theorien der Wissenschaftsgeschichte: Beiträge zur diachronen Wissenschaftstheorie*. Frankfurt am Main: Suhrkamp, 1974.

Dijksterhuis, E. J. *The Mechanization of the World Picture: Pythagoras to Newton*. Trans-lated by C. Dikshoorn. Oxford: Clarendon Press, 1961. Dutch ed. *De mechanisering van het wereldbeeld*. Amsterdam, 1950.

101

Dijksterhuis, E. J., and R. J. Forbes. *Overwinning door gehoorzaamheid: geschiedenis van natuurwetenschap en techniek.* 2 vols. Antwerp: De Haan, 1961.

Dolman, H. "Theoriekeuze in Weimar Duitsland: de neurologie van Kurt Goldstein." *Kennis en methode* 8 (1984): 4–16.

Dooyeweerd, H. *De crisis der humanistische staatsleer in het licht eener calvinistische kosmologie en kennistheorie.* Amsterdam: Ten Have, 1931.

————. *De wijsbegeerte der wetsidee.* 3 vols. Amsterdam: Paris, 1935, 1935, 1936.

————. "De transcendentale critiek van het wijsgeerig denken en de grondslagen van de wijsgeerige denkgemeenschap van het avondland." *Philosophia Reformata* 6 (1941): 1–20.

————. *A New Critique of Theoretical Thought.* Translated by D. H. Freeman and W. S. Young. 4 vols. Philadelphia: Presbyterian and Reformed, 1953, 1955, 1957, 1958.

————. "Schepping en evolutie." *Philosophia Reformata* 24 (1959): 113–59.

————. *Roots of Western Culture: Pagan, Secular and Christian Options.* Toronto: Wedge, 1979.

Drake, Stillman. *Discoveries and Opinions of Galileo.* New York: Doubleday Anchor, 1957. (English translation of *The Assayer*, p. 229–280).

Duijker, Hubertus C. J. *Psychopolis: een essay over de beoefening der psychologie.* Deventer: Van Loghum Slaterus, 1980.

Eekhof, Albert. *De zinspreuk "In necessariis unitas, in non necessariis libertas in utrisque caritas. . ."* Leiden: Sijthoff, 1931.

Eisler, R. E. *Wörterbuch der Philosophischen Begriffe.* Berlin: Mittler, 1927 (A–K), 1929 (L–Sch), 1930 (Sci–Z).

Einstein, Albert. "Science and Religion." In his *Ideas and Opinions.* New York: Bonanza (1954): 41–49.

Encylopedia of Philosophy. 8 vols. Edited by P. Edwards. New York, 1967.

Fiorenza, F.P., and J. B. Metz. "De mens als eenheid van lichaam en ziel." In *Mysterium salutis: dogmatiek in heilshistorisch perspectief.* Edited by J. Feiner and M. Löhrer. Vol. 8. Hilversum: Paul Brand (1968): 42–112.

Figlio, K. M. "The Metaphor of Organization: A Historiographical Perspective on the Biomedical Sciences of the Early 19th Century." *History of Science* 14 (1976): 17–53.

Foucault, M. "Ervaring en waarheid." *See:* Trombadori 1985.

————. *The Order of Things: An Archaeology of Human Sciences.* New York: Vintage, 1970. (Original French ed. 1966).

Fretz, L. *Ethiek als wetenschap.* Meppel: Boom, 1980.

Gay, Peter. *The Enlightenment: An Interpretation, Vol. 1 The Rise of Modern Paganism.* New York: Knopf, 1967.

Geertsema, Henk G. *Van boven naar voren.* Kampen: Kok, 1980.

Gillespie, Neal C. *Charles Darwin and the Problem of Creation.* Chicago: University of Chicago Press, 1979.

Gogarten, Friedrich. *Verhängnis und Hoffnung der Neuzeit: Der Säkularisierung als theologisches Problem.* Stuttgart: Vorwerk, 1953.

Goldenson, A. "Een joodse visie op de verhouding van God, mens en wereld." In *Zoals er gezegd is over de schepping.* Vol. 1. The Hague: Phoenix, 1962.

Gombrich, Ernst H. *In Search of Cultural History*. Oxford: Clarendon Press, 1978.

"The Gospel of Thomas." In *The Nag Hammadi Library in English*. Translated by Thomas O. Lambdin. Edited by James Robinson and Richard Smith. 3rd rev. edition. Leiden: Brill (1988): 124ff.

Gould, Stephen J. *Ontogeny and Phylogeny*. Cambridge, MA: Harvard University Press, 1977.

Griffin, D. A. *A Process Christology*. Lanham: University of America Press, 1990.

Griffioen, Sander. "Newbegins cultuurfilosofie." In *Het evangelie in het westen*. Edited by M. E. Brinkman and H. Noordegraaf. Kampen: Kok, 1990, 49–60.

Griffioen, Sander, and Bert M. Balk, eds. *Christian Philosophy at the Close of the Twentieth Century*. Kampen: Kok, 1995.

Groen van Prinsterer, Guillaume. *Bescheiden*. Edited by J. Zwaan. 's-Gravenhage, 1990–1991. Schriftelijke Nalatenschap, vols. 8 and 9. Rijksgeschiedkundige Publicatiën (RGP), Grote Serie 209, 210.

Grote Winkler Prins. 5th ed. 25 vols. Amsterdam, Elsevier, 1979–1984.

Haitjema, T. L., H. Schokking and J. Ch. Kromsigt. *Christusprediking tegenover moderne gnostiek*. Wageningen: Veenman, 1929.

Hart, Hendrik. "De probleem-historische methode van Prof. Dr. D. H. Th. Vollenhoven." *Correspondentie-bladen van de Vereniging voor Calvinistische Wijsbegeerte* 29 (November 1965): 3–15.

———. *Communal Certainty and Authorized Truth: An Examination of John Dewey's Philosophy of Verification*. Amsterdam. Swets and Zeitlinger, 1966.

———. *Understanding Our World. An Integral Ontology*. Lanham. University Press of America, 1984.

Hartmann, Nicolai. "Das Problem der Apriorismus in der Platonischen Philosophie" (1935). In *Kleinere Schriften II. Abhandlungen zur Philosophie-Geschicht*. Berlin: De Gruyter, 1957: 48-84.

Heimsoeth, H. *The Six Great Themes of Western Metaphysics*. (1922) Detroit: Wayne State University, 1994.

Heindel, Max. *The Rosicrucian Cosmo-conception*. 10th ed. Oceanside, CA: Rosicrucian Fellowship, 1925.

Hemleben, Johannes. *Oerbegin en Werelddoel*, Rotterdam: Christofoor, 1979.

Henderson, Roger D. *Illuminating Law: The Construction of Herman Dooyeweerd's Philosophy 1918–1928*. PhD diss. Vrije Universiteit, 1994.

Hergenhahn, B. R. *An Introduction to the History of Psychology*. 3rd ed. Pacific Grove, CA: Brooks/Cole, 1997.

Hermans, W. F. "Otto Weininger's *Geschlect und Charakter* vertaald" *NRC-H* July 27, 1984.

Historisches Wörterbuch der Philosophie (HWP). 12 vols. Edited by Joachim Ritter and K. Gründer. Darmstadt: Wissenschaftliche Buchgesellschaft, 1971–2005.

Hocking, W. Ernest. *Types of Philosophy*. New York: Scribner, 1929. (Rev. ed. 1939.)

Hommes, H. J. *Een nieuwe herleving van het natuurrecht*. Zwolle: Willink, 1961.

Hooykaas, R. *Geschiedenis der natuurwetenschappen*. 2nd ed. Utrecht, 1976.

Hoppe, Brigitte. "Polarität, Stufung und Metamorphose in der spekulativen Biologie." *Naturwiss. Rundschau* 20 (1967): 380–83.

Horkheimer, Max, and Theodor W. Adorno. *Dialectic of Enlightenment* (1944). Translated by John Cumming. New York: Herder and Herder: 1972.

Husserl, Edmund. *Die Krisis der Europäischen Wissenschaften und die tranzendentale Phänomenologie.* The Hague: Nijhoff, 1954.

HWP. See: *Historisches Wörterbuch der Philosophie.*

Jongeneel, J. A. B. *Het redelijk geloof in Jezus Christus.* Wageningen: Veenman, 1971.

Jung, Carl Gustav. *Collected Works* (CW). 20 vols. London: Routledge, 1970–1979.

Kamphuis, J. "De mens: schepsel en beeld van God." In *In het licht van Genesis.* Edited by A. P. Wisse. Barneveld: Vuurbaak, 1986.

Kant, Immanuel. *Critique of Practical Reason.* Translated by L. W. Beck. Indianapolis: Bobbs-Merrill, 1956.

Kelly, J. N. D. *Early Christian Creeds.* London: Longman, 1972.

Kenney, John P. *Mystical Monotheism: A Study in Ancient Platonic Theology.* Hanover: University Press of New England, 1991.

Klapwijk, J. "In memoriam." *Kerkblad G. K. Amsterdam,* June 17, 1978, 5.

———. "Reformational Philosophy on the Boundary between the Past and the Future," *Philosophia Reformata* 52/2 (1987): 101–35.

Kok, John H. *Vollenhoven: His Early Development.* Sioux Center: Dordt College Press, 1992.

Koningsveld, Herman. *Het verschijnsel wetenschap.* Meppel, 1976.

Kuhn, Helmut. "German Philosophy and National Socialism," in *Encyclopedia of Philosophy* 3 (1967): 309–316.

Kuhn, Thomas S. *The Copernican Revolution: Planetary Astronomy in the Development of Western Thought.* Cambridge, MA: Harvard University Press, 1957.

———. *The Structure of Scientific Revolutions.* 2nd ed. Chicago: University of Chicago Press, 1970.

———. *The Essential Tension: Selected Studies in Scientific Traditions and Change.* Chicago: University of Chicago Press, 1977.

Kuypers, K. *Immanuel Kant.* Baarn: Wereldvenster, 1966.

Lack, David L. *Evolutionary Theory and Christian Belief: The Unresolved Conflict.* London: Methuen, 1957.

Lambrechts, Mark. *Michel Foucault: excerpten en kritieken.* Nijmegen: Socialistische Uitgeverij, 1982.

Laudan, Larry. *Progress and Its Problems: Toward a Theory of Scientific Growth.* Berkeley: University of California Press, 1977.

Lemaire, Ton. *Het vertoog over de ongelijkheid van Jean-Jacques Rousseau.* Baarn: Ambo, 1980.

Lietaert Peerholte, M. *Psychocybernetica.* Amsterdam: Bezige Bij, 1968.

———. *De verschijning mens.* Amsterdam: Bezige Bij, 1971.

———. *Poimandres.* Deventer: Ankh-Hermes, 1974.

Lindberg, David C. *The Beginning of Western Science.* Chicago: University of Chicago Press, 1992.

Lock, G. E. "Politieke ideologie." *Intermediair* 17 nr. 3 (March 27, 1981).

Locke, John. *An Essay Concerning Human Understanding.* Oxford: Clarendon, 1975.

Löwith, Karl. "Max Weber und seine Nachfolger." In *Mass und Wert* 3, 1940, 166–76.

Mandelbaum, M. "The History of Ideas, Intellectual History, and History of Philosophy." *History and Theory;* suppl. 5 (1965): 33–66.

Mantz-van der Meer, A. E. G. *Op zoek naar loutering: oorsprong en ontwikkeling van de enkratistische ascese tot het begin van de 13^e eeuw.* Hilversum: Verloren, 1989.

McGrath, Alister E. *A Passion for Truth: The Intellectual Coherence of Evangelism.* Leicester: Apollos, 1996.

Meinema, D. "God en wereld in beweging." *Beweging* 53 (February 1989): 10–13.

Mendelsohn, Everett., ed. *Transformation and Tradition in Science: Essays in Honor of I. Bernard Cohen.* Cambridge: Cambridge University Press, 1985.

Merlan, Phillip. *From Platonism to Neoplatonism.* 2nd. rev. ed. The Hague: Nijhoff, 1960.

———. *Kleine philosophische Schriften.* Hildesheim: Olms, 1976.

Merquior, J. G. *Foucault.* Berkeley: University of California Press, 1985.

Meuleman, G. E. "Herleving van de natuurlijke theologie in Amerika." *Gereformeerd Theologisch Tijdschrift* 74 (February 1974): 49–71.

Monk, R. *Ludwig Wittgenstein.* London: Vintage, 1991.

Mossner, E. C. "Herbert of Cherbury." *Encyclopedia of Philosophy* 3 (1967): 484–486.

Nelson, John O. "Innate Ideas." *Encyclopedia of Philosophy* 4 (1967): 196–198.

Nietzsche, Friedrich. *"The Antichrist."* In *The Portable Nietzsche.* Translated and edited by W. Kaufmann. New York, 1954.

———. *Werke in drei Bände.* Edited by K. Schlechta. München: Hanser, 1956.

———. *Ecco Homo.* Translated and edited by W. Kaufmann. New York: Vintage, 1967.

Nijk, A. J. *Secularisatie.* Rotterdam: Lemniscaat, 1968.

Noordegraaf, A. *Leven voor Gods aangezicht: gedachten over het mens-zijn.* Kampen: Kok, 1990.

O'Connell, Marvin. *Blaise Pascal: Reasons of the Heart.* Grand Rapids: Eerdmans, 1997.

O'Regan, C. *Gnostic Return in Modernity.* New York: SUNY, 2001.

OE. See: *Oosthoeks Encyclopedie.* 5th ed. 1959–1964.

Oosterhoff, B. J. *De ondergang van Israël en Juda.* Kampen: Kok, 1981.

Oosthoek's Encyclopaedie. 4th ed. Utrecht: Oosthoek, 1947–1957, 15 vols. Cf. Voll 49f.

Oosthoeks Encyclopedie (OE). 5th ed. Utrecht: Oosthoek, 1959–1964, 15 vols. Cf. Voll 59f.

Oosthuizen, Jacobus S. *Van Plotinus tot Teilhard de Chardin.* Amsterdam: Rodopi, 1974.

Ouweneel, Willem J. "Zie hoe alles hier verandert. . . ." *Radix* 17 (1991): 208–46.

Pagels, Elaine H. *The Gnostic Gospels.* New York: Vintage, 1981.

Parabirsing, S. T. *De metabletische methode: een analyse van de leer van J. H. van den Berg.* Meppel: Boom, 1974.

Peeters, H. F. M. *Historische gedragswetenschap.* Meppel: Boom, 1978.

Peperzak, Adriaan T. "Filosofie." In *Woordenboek Filosofie.* Edited by W. H. M. Willemsen. Assen: Van Gorcum (1992): 154-57.

Phillips, Derek L. *De naakte Nederlander: kritische overpeinzingen.* Amsterdam: Bakker, 1985.

Poortman, J. J. *Vehicles of Cconsciousness: The Concept of Hylic Pluralism (Ochêma).* 4 vols. Wheaton, IL: Theosophical, 1978.

105

Popma, Klaas J. "Hoofd- en nevenrichtingen in het realisme." *Correspondentie Bladen van de Vereniging voor Calvinistische Wijsbegeerte.* 6 nr. 3 (September 1941): 50–51.
———. "Historicale methode en historische continuïteit." *Philosophia Reformata* 17 (1952): 97–145.
———. *Levensbeschouwing.* 7 vols. Amsterdam, 1958–1965.
———. *Wijsbegeerte en anthropologie.* Amsterdam, 1963.
Popper, Karl R. "Natural Reflection and the Emergence of Mind." *Dialectica* 32 (1978): 339–55.
Popper, Karl R., and John C. Eccles. *The Self and Its Brain.* Berlin: Springer, 1977.
Praamsma, L. *De kerk van alle tijden.* 4 vols. Franeker, 1979–1981.
Quispel, Gilles, ed. *Gnosis. De derde component van de Europese cultuurtraditie.* 2nd edition. Utrecht: HES, 1988.
———. *Het evangelie van Thomas en de Nederlanden.* Baarn: Tirion, 1991.
Quispel, Gilles, and H. Verkerk. *De verliezers.* Arnhem: Interlektuur, 1981.
Radder, Hans. "Kramers en de Formanthesen." *Kennis en methode* 6 (1982): 313–333.
Religion (Die) in Geschichte und Gegenwart (RGG). 3rd edition. Tübingen: Mohr, 1957–1965.
RGG. See: *Religion in Geschichte und Gegenwart.*
Rickert, Heinrich. *Die Philosophie des Lebens.* Tübingen: Mohr, 1920.
Rider, J., and N. Leser, ed. *Otto Weininger.* Vienna: Oesterreichischer Bundesverlage, 1984.
Ries, Wiebrecht. *Friedrich Nietzsche.* Hannover: Schlüter, 1977.
Roessingh, Karel H. *De moderne theologie in Nederland: hare voorbereiding en eerste periode.* Groningen: Van der kamp, 1914.
———. *Verzamelde werken.* 4 vols. Arnhem, 1926–1929.
Romein, Jan. *Op het breukvlak van twee eeuwen.* Amertdam: Querido, 1967.
———. *Historische lijnen en patronen.* Amsterdam: Querido, 1971.
Rousseau, Jean-Jacques. *Discourse on the Origin of Inequality.* [1755] Translated by D. A. Cress. Indianapolis: Hackett, 1992.
Rudolph, Kurt. *Gnosis: The Nature and History of Gnosticism.* San Francisco: Harper and Row, 1987.
Runia, D. T. "Plato, de eerste grote filosoof." In *Grote filosofen.* Edited by J. Davidse. Kampen: Kok (1991): 17-38.
Ruse, Michael E. *The Darwinian Revolution. Science Red in Tooth and Claws.* Chicago: University of Chicago Press, 1979.
Russell, Bertrand. "My Mental Development." In *The Philosophy of Bertrand Russell.* Edited by Paul A. Schilpp. 3rd edition. New York: Tudor, 1951): 3–20.
Sanders, C., and J. F. H. van Rappard. "Psychological or Philosophical Issues? Reply to Commentators." In *Annals of Theoretical Psychology* 3 New York: Plenum (1985): 291–296.
Sartre, Jean P. "Existentialism Is a Humanism." In *Existentialism from Dostoevsky to Sartre.* Edited by W. Kaufmann. New York: Meridian (1956): 287–311.
Sassen, Ferdinand L. R. *Geschiedenis van de nieuwere wijsbegeerte tot Kant.* 2nd rev. ed. Antwerp: Standaard, 1946.
———. *Thomas van Aquino.* 2nd rev. ed. The Hague: Krusemas, 1961.

Sassen, Ferdinand L. R., and B. Delfgaauw. *Wijsbegeerte van onze tijd.* 4th rev. ed. Antwerp: Standaard, 1957.

Schierbeek, Abraham. *Goethe als natuuronderzoeker.* Amsterdam: Meulenhoff, 1944.

Schilder, Klaas. *De Kerk.* Goes: Oosterbaan en LeCointre, 1960.

Schippers, R., and T. Baarda. *Het evangelie van Thomas.* Kampen: Kok, 1960.

Schoeps, Hans-J. *Was ist und was will die Geistesgeschichte? Ueber Theorie und Praxis der Zeitgeistforschung.* Göttingen: Musterschmidt, 1959.

Scholem, Gershom. *Major Trends in Jewish Mysticism.* 3rd ed. New York: Schocken, 1954.

———. *Kabbalah.* New York: Quadrangle, 1974.

Seerveld, Calvin G. (1965) "Dooyeweerd's Contribution to the Historiography of Philosophy." In *Philosophy and Christianity: philosophical essays dedicated to Professor Dr. Herman Dooyeweerd.* Kampen: Kok, 1965, 193–202.

———. "Biblical Wisdom underneath Vollenhoven's Categories for Philosophical Historiography." *Philosophia Reformata* 38 (1973): 127–43.

Smit, Meyer C. *Toward a Christian Conception of History.* Edited and translated by Herbert Donald Morton and Harry Van Dyke. Lanham: University Press of America, 2002.

Solmsen, Friedrich. "Plato and the Concept of the Soul." *Journal of the History of Ideas* 44 (1983): 355–67.

Spitzer, L. "*Geistesgeschichte* vs. History of Ideas as Applied to Hitlerism." *Journal of the History of Ideas* 5 (1944): 191–203.

Spoelstra, T. A. Th. *Sterrekunde in de geschiedenis.* Goes: Oosterbaan en LeCointre, 1979.

Sprague, Elmer. "Paley, William." In *Encyclopedia of Philosophy* 6 (1967): 19–20

———. "Shaftesbury." In *Encyclopedia of Philosophy* 7 (1967): 428–430.

Staff, Ilse, ed. *Justiz im dritten Reich.* Frankfurt am Main: Fischer, 1964.

Stellingwerff, Johannes. *D. H. Th. Vollenhoven (1892–1978) Reformator der wijsbegeerte.* Baarn: Ten Have, 1992.

———. "Vollenhoven, Dirk Hendrik Theodoor." In *Biografisch lexicon voor de geschiedenis van het Nederlandse protestantisme.* Kampen: Kok. 5 (2001): 542–45.

Steubing, Hans, ed. *Bekenntnisse der Kirche.* 2nd edition. Wuppertal: Brockhaus, 1977.

Störig, Hans J. *Geschiedenis van de filosofie.* 2 vols. Utrecht: Spectrum, 1959.

Struyker Boudier, H. M. A. *Inleiding in het mediese denken van J. H. van den Berg en M. Foucault.* Nijmegen: SUN, 1975.

Theiler, W. *Die Vorbereitung der Neuplatonismus.* Berlin: Weidmann, 1930.

Thévenaz, Pierre. *La condition de la raison philosophique.* Neuchâtel: Baconnière, 1960.

Tol, Anthony. "Vollenhoven en het postmoderne." *Beweging* 56, no. 3 (June 1992): 52–55.

———. "Vollenhovens probleemhistorische methode tegen de achtergrond van zijn systematisch denken." *Philosophia Reformata* 58, no. 1 (1993): 2–27.

———. (2003a) "On Translating Vollenhoven's Term: 'Consequent-probleemhistorische methode.'" *Vollenhoven Newsletter.* 1 (July 2003): 5–9. Email journal: <http://home.wxs.nl/~srw>

———. (2003b) "Vollenhoven en de wijsbegeerte van de wiskunde." *Beweging* 67, no. 2 (2003): 42–43.

Tol, Anthony, and Kornelis A. Bril. *Vollenhoven als wijsgeer: Inleidingen en teksten.* Amsterdam: Buijten en Schipperheijn, 1992.

Torrey, Norman L. "Diderot." In *Encyclopedia of Philosophy* 2 (1967): 397–403.

Trombadori, D. *Ervaring en waarheid. Trombadori in gesprek met Foucault.* Stichting Te Elfder Ure, 1985.

Turner, Stephen P., and Regis A. Factor. *Max Weber and the Dispute over Reason and Value.* London: Routledge and Kegan, 1984.

Ueberweg, Friedrich. *Grundriss der Geschichte der Philosophie.* 5 vols. Berlin: Mittler, 1924–1928.

Underhill, Evelyn. *Mysticism: A Study in the Nature and Development of Man's Spiritual Consciousness.* 12th ed. New York: Meridian, 1955.

Van den Berg, Jan H. *De betekenis van de phaenomenologische of existentiële anthropologie in de psychiatrie.* Utrecht: Kemink, 1946.

———. *Metabletica.* Nijkerk: Callenbach, 1956. [English translation: *The Changing Nature of Man.* New York: Norton, 1961.]

———. *Het menselijk lichaam: een metabletisch onderzoek.* 2 vols. Nijkerk: Callenbach, 1959 and 1961.

———. *Metabletica van de materie.* Nijkerk: Callenbach, 1968.

———. *Gedane Zaken.* Nijkerk, Callenbach, 1977.

———. *Koude rillingen over de rug van Charles Darwin.* Nijkerk: Callenbach, 1984.

———. *Hooligans.*Nijkerk: Callenbach, 1989

Van den Beukel, A. *More Things in Heaven and Earth: God and the Scientists.* Translated by John Bowden. London: SCM Press, 1991.

Van der Bercken, W. *De intellectuele herwaardering van het Christendom in de Sovjet-Unie.* Vught: Radboudstichting, 1989.

Van der Heyden, M. C. A., ed. *Ik wou zo graag verstandig wezen. Geschriften uit de sfeer der Verlichting.* Utrecht: Spektrum, 1968.

———.*Gevoelige harten. Schetsen en verhalen in de ban der Romantiek.* Utrecht: Spektrum: 1969.

Van der Steen, W. J. "Ethiek een algemene wetenschap?" *Filosofie en Praktijk,* 12/3 (1991): 125–137.

Van der Walt, Bennie J. *Horizon: Surveying a Route for Contemporary Christian Thought.* Potchefstroom, 1978.

Van Dijk, Arie J. (Harry Van Dyke). "Verlichting en secularisatie." *Beweging* 53 no. 6 (December 1989): 103–6.

———. "Gods oordelen in de geschiedenis." *Beweging* 55 no. 6 (December 1991): 103–5.

Van Dongen, H., and J. L. F. Gerding. *PSI in wetenschap en wijsbegeerte.* Deventer: Ankh-Hermes, 1983.

Van Genderen, J., and W. H. Velema. *Beknopte Gereformeerde Dogmatiek.* Kampen: Kok, 1992.

Van Helsdingen, R. J. *C. G. Jung.* 4th ed. The Hague: Kruseman, 1983.

Van Hoorn, W. C. L. *Ancient and Modem Theories of Visual Perception.* Amsterdam: University Press, 1972.

Van Nieuwenburg, C. J. *Korte geschiedenis van de chemie.* Hilversum: Centen, 1961.

Van Schaik, J. L. M. *Unde Malum—Vanwaar het kwaad? Dualisme bij manicheeërs en katharen. Een vergelijkend onderzoek.* Baarn: Ten Have, 2004.

Van Wersch, S. *De gnostisch-occulte vloedgolf.* Kampen: Kok, 1990.

Verburg, Marcel E. *Herman Dooyeweerd: Leven en werk van een Nederlands Christen-wijsgeer.* Baarn: Ten Have, 1989.

Visee, G. *Onderwezen in het Koninkrijk der hemelen.* 2 vols. Kampen: Van den Berg, 1979, 1982.

Vollenhoven Newsletter. No. 1, July 2003. Email journal.

Vollenhoven, Dirk H. Th.: The enumeration given below (1918a, etc.) is according to John Kok (1992).

――――. (1918a) *De wijsbegeerte der wiskunde van theïstisch standpunt.* Amsterdam: Van Soest, 1918.

――――. (1933a) *Het Calvinisme en de reformatie van de wijsbegeerte.* Amsterdam: Paris, 1933.

――――. (1938v) "Realisme en nominalisme." *Philosophia Reformata* 3 (1938): 65–83, 150–65.

――――. (1941k) "Richtlijnen ter oriëntatie in de gangbare wijsbegeerte." *Philosophia Reformata* 6 (1941): 65–86; 7 (1942): 946; 8 (1943): 1–33.

――――. (1943a) *Isagoogè Philosophiae.* Amsterdam: Theja. (Cf. 1967b; see: 2005a for translation).

――――. (1949f) Articles in *Oosthoek's encyclopaedie.* 4th ed. Utrecht: Oosthoek, 1947–1957. (cf. 1959f).

――――. (1950e) *Geschiedenis der Wijsbegeerte. I. Inleiding en geschiedenis der Griekse wijsbegeerte voor Plato en Aristoteles.* Franeker: Wever, 1950. (English translation see: 1958a).

――――. (1955ms) *Levens-eenheid.* Lecture given at Utrecht 1955. (Included in Voll 1992.)

――――. (1956b) *Kort Overzicht van de geschiedenis der wijsbegeerte voor de Cursus paedagogiek.* Amsterdam: Theja, 1956. (English translation in Voll 2005b).

――――. (1958a) *"The History of Ancient Philosophy."* Translated by H.Evan Runner. Grand Rapids, MI: Calvin College, 1958. (A translation of the first 312 pages of Voll 1950e.)

――――. (1958d) Student Lecture Notes: *Typologie (Wijsgerige anthropologie).* (1958–1959).

――――. (1959a) "Conservatisme en progressiviteit in de wijsbegeerte." In *Conservatisme en progressiviteit in de wetenschap.* Kampen: Kok, 1959, 35–48. (English translation in Voll 2005b).

――――. (1959f) Articles in *Oosthoeks Encyclopedie.* 5th ed. 15 vols. Utrecht: Oosthoek. 1959–1964. See: Voll 2005c.

――――. (1961c) "De consequent probleemhistorische methode." *Philosophia Reformata. 26* (1961): 1–34. (English translation in Voll 2005b).

――――. (1962d) *Schematische kaarten, met register, behorend bij: Kort overzicht van de geschiedenis der westerse wijsbegeerte.* Amsterdam: Free University, 1962. 2nd rev. ed. Voll 2000.

――――. (1963a) "Plato's realisme." *Philosophia Reformata* 28 (1963): 97–133. (In part in Voll 1992).

————. (1963b) *Het probleem van de tijd.* College systematiek, 1963. (Manuscript. Included in Voll 1992).

————. (1964a) "Hoofdtrekken der wijsgerige problematiek in de hedendaagse mensbeschouwing." *Koers, maandblad vir Calvinistiese Denke,* 32 (1964, 5 and 6): 189–219. (In Voll 1992).

————. (1965a) "Methode perikelen bij de Parmenides-interpretatie." *Philosophia Reformata* 30 (1965): 63–112.

————. (1967b) *Isagoogè Philosophiae.* Amsterdam: Filosofisch Instituut, Free University, 1967. (The same text as 1943a; see: 2005a for translation.)

————. (1970a) "Historische achtergrond en toekomst." *Mededelingen v.d. Vereniging voor Calvinistische Wijsbegeerte* (December 1970): 2–3.

————. (1971a) *Privatissimum* 1970/1971. Amsterdam: Filosofisch Instituut, Free University, 1971.

————. (1979a) *D. H. Th. Vollenhoven: Ancient Philosophical Conceptions in Problem-Historical Lay-out, 6th Century B.C.–6th Century A.D.* Edited with an introduction by A. Tol. Amsterdam: Filosofisch Instituut, Free University, 1979.

————. (1982a) *Vollenhoven's laatste werk.* Edited with an introduction by K. A. Bril. Amsterdam: Free University Boekhandel, 1982. (Contains the private lecture series between 1970 and 1975).

————. (1992) In *Vollenhoven als wijsgeer. Inleidingen en teksten.* Edited by A. Tol and K. A. Bril. Amsterdam: Buijten en Schipperheijn, 1992. (Contains, among other articles, Vollenhoven 1959a, 1963a, 1963b, 1964a, 1968b.)

————. (2000) *Schematisch Kaarten. Filosofische Concepties in Probleemhistorisch verband.* Edited by K. A. Bril and P. J. Boonstra. Amstelveen: De Zaak Haes, 2000.

————. (2005a) *Isagôgè Philosophiae: Introduction to Philosophy.* Edited by John H. Kok and Anthony Tol. Sioux Center, Iowa: Dordt College Press, 2005.

————. (2005b). *The Problem-Historical Method and the History of Philosophy.* Edited by K. A. Bril. (Contains the following publications: Vollenhoven 1956b, 1959a, 1961c, and 1965c.)

————. (2005c). *Wijsgerig Woordenboek* [Philosophical Dictionary] Edited by K. A. Bril. Amstelveen, 2005. This volume collects the philosophical articles that Vollenhoven wrote for the fifteen-volume *Oosthoek Encyclopedie.* 5th ed. 1959–1964. (Voll 1959f).

————. (2005d) *A Vollenhoven Reader.* Edited by John H. Kok. Sioux Center, IA: Dordt College Press, 2005.

Vonk, C. *De Heilige Schrift.* Barendrecht: Liebeek en Hooimeijer, 1960.

Von Rad, G. "Die biblische Schöpfungsgeschichte." In *Schöpfungsglaube und Evolutionstheorie.* Edited by Ludwig von Bertalanfy. Stuttgart: Köner (1955): 25–37.

Vree, J. *De Groninger godgeleerden: de oorsprong en de eerste periode van hun optreden (1820–1843).* Kampen: Kok, 1984.

Vunderink, Ralph W. "Review of Dooyeweerd's *Roots of Western Culture,* 1979." *Calvin Theological Journal* 15, no. 2 (1980): 268–73.

————. "Review of M. E. Verburg's *Herman Dooyeweerd,* 1990." *Calvin Theological Journal* 29, no. 1 (1994): 221–26.

———. "Ground Motifs: A Modest Revision." In *Contemporary Reflections on the Philosophy of Herman Dooyeweerd*. Edited by D. F. M. Strauss and Michelle Botting. Lewiston, NY: Edwin Mellin Press (2000): 157–77.

Walgrave, J. H. "Recensie." *Tijdschrift voor Filosofie* 39 (1981): 538.

Weininger, Otto. *Geschlecht und Charakter: eine prinzipielle Untersuchung.* Berlin: Kiepenheuer, 1932.

Wetlesen, Jon. ed. *Spinoza's Philosophy of Man.* Oslo Universitetforl., 1978.

Whitehead, Alfred N. *Science and the Modern World.* New York: Macmillan, 1925.

———. *Process and Reality* (1929) New York: Harper, 1960.

Wildiers, N.M. (Max). *Theologie op nieuwe wegen.* Kampen: Kok. 1985.

Wiles, Maurice. *The Making of the Christian Doctrine.* Cambridge: Cambridge University Press, 1975.

Winter, U. *Der Materialismus bei Diderot.* Geneve, 1972.

Wissink, J. B. *The Eternity of the World in the Thought of Thomas Aquinas and His Receptors.* Leiden: Brill, 1990.

Wolfson, Harry A. *Philo: Foundations of Religious Philosophy in Judaism, Christianity, and Islam.* Vol. I. Cambridge, MA: Harvard University Press, 1947.

———. *The Philosophy of the Church Fathers.* Vol. 1. *Faith, Trinity, Incarnation.* Cambridge, MA: Harvard University Press, 1956.

Wolters, Albert M. *Creation Regained: Biblical Basics for a Reformational Worldview.* Grand Rapids: Eerdmans, 1985.

Wytzes, J. *Plato's Phaedo.* The Hague: Christelijk Paedagogisch Studiecentrum, 1960.

Yates, Frances A. *Giordano Bruno and the Hermetic Tradition.* Chicago: University of Chicago Press, 1978.

Zandee, Jan. *Het evangelie der waarheid: een gnostisch geschrift.* Amsterdam: TenHave, 1965.

Zijlstra, Onno K. *Authenticiteit en vervreemding. Filosofie en cultuurkritiek van José Ortega y Gasset.* Amsterdam: VUB, 1982.

Zuidema, Sietse U. *Nacht zonder Dageraad.* Franeker: Wever. 1948.

———. *Communisme in Ontbinding.* Wageningen: Zomer en Keuning, 1957.

———. "Vollenhoven en de reformatie der wijsbegeerte." *Philosophia Reformata* 28 (1963): 134–46.

Zwaan, Johan. "Groen van Prinsterer over de wijsbegeerte." *Correspondentie. Bladen van de Vereniging voor Calvinistische Wijsbegeert* 36, no. 2 (September 1972): 29–45.

———. *Groen van Prinsterer en de klassieke oudheid.* Amsterdam: Hakkert, 1973.

———. (1990–91) *See:* Groen van Prinsterer. *Bescheiden.* 1990, 1991.

Zwart, Hub. *Boude bewoordingen: de historische fenomenologie ('metabletica') van Jan Hendrik van den Berg.* Kampen: Klement, 2002.

Subject Index

* Typological categories are italicized; time-currents (periods) are underlined.

Name Index